SDI and U.S.
Foreign Policy

The Johns Hopkins Foreign Policy Institute (FPI) was founded in 1980 and serves as the research center for the School of Advanced International Studies (SAIS) in Washington, D.C. The FPI is a meeting place for SAIS faculty members and students as well as for government analysts, policymakers, diplomats, journalists, business leaders, and other specialists in international affairs. In addition to conducting research on policy-related international issues, the FPI sponsors conferences, seminars, and roundtables.

The FPI's research activities are often carried out in conjunction with SAIS's regional and functional programs dealing with Latin America and the Caribbean Basin, U.S. foreign policy, U.S.-Japan relations, Canada, Africa, Europe, security studies, international energy, and international economics.

FPI publications include the *SAIS Review*, a biannual journal of foreign affairs, which is edited by SAIS students; the SAIS Papers in International Affairs, a monograph series copublished with Westview Press in Boulder, Colorado; the FPI Policy Briefs, a series of analyses of immediate or emerging foreign-policy issues; and the FPI Case Studies, a series designed to teach analytical negotiating skills.

SDI and U.S. Foreign Policy is the fourth in a series of five books. This series is being prepared by the FPI as part of a research project on the long-term implications of military programs and activities in space for strategic stability, superpower relations, and alliance cohesion.

For additional information regarding FPI publications, write to: FPI Publications Program, School of Advanced International Studies, The Johns Hopkins University, 1740 Massachusetts Avenue, N.W., Washington, D.C. 20036.

ABOUT THE BOOK AND AUTHORS

Showing how the development of space technology could affect the present system of deterrence, the authors consider the consequences for U.S. foreign policy, alliance relations, and strategic stability. In the first essay, Dr. Tucker argues that a greater commitment to defensive systems would not substantially affect deterrence or extended deterrence. Rather, if attainable, a ballistic missile defense (BMD) capability would only alter the character of our vulnerability to nuclear weapons. Dr. Liska suggests that a new offense-defense mix might enhance deterrence because of the greater uncertainty of military outcomes. He warns, though, that one side might risk a first strike if it perceives that the other is about to achieve invulnerability.

European responses to SDI are examined by Dr. Osgood, who maintains that the issue of defensive shields could become the chief obstacle to establishing a more stable offense-defense weapons mix acceptable to the allies. Although Europeans perceive technological benefits from a limited initiative, they are committed to a strategy of flexible response, safeguarded by the ABM treaty. In Dr. Calleo's view, the strategic dilemma of the United States can be improved only through a devolution of security responsibility. He argues that it is unrealistic to rely on a nuclear strategy that seeks to solve geopolitical problems through technology and stresses that Europe must gradually assume primary responsibility for its own defense.

Robert W. Tucker is the Edward B. Burling Professor of International Law and Institutions at SAIS. **George Liska** is professor of political science at The Johns Hopkins University. **David P. Calleo** is professor and director of European studies at SAIS.

Robert E. Osgood, who was the Christian A. Herter Professor of American Foreign Policy at SAIS, passed away shortly before publication of this book, which his coauthors wish to dedicate to his memory.

SAIS
PAPERS IN INTERNATIONAL AFFAIRS

SDI and U.S.
Foreign Policy

Robert W. Tucker
George Liska
Robert E. Osgood
David P. Calleo

WESTVIEW PRESS/BOULDER AND LONDON
WITH THE FOREIGN POLICY INSTITUTE
SCHOOL OF ADVANCED INTERNATIONAL STUDIES
THE JOHNS HOPKINS UNIVERSITY

A Westview Press / Foreign Policy Institute Edition

This Westview softcover edition is printed on acid-free paper and bound in softcovers that carry the highest rating of the National Association of State Textbook Administrators, in consultation with the Association of American Publishers and the Book Manufacturers' Institute.

Published in 1987 in the United States of America by Westview Press, Inc.; Frederick A. Praeger, Publisher; 5500 Central Avenue, Boulder, Colorado 80301

Library of Congress Catalog Card Number: 86-51674
ISBN 0-8133-0468-7

Composition for this book was provided by The Magazine Group, Inc., Washington, D.C., for The Johns Hopkins Foreign Policy Institute, SAIS.
This book was produced without formal editing by the publisher.

Printed and bound in the United States of America

The paper used in this publication meets the requirements of the American National Standard for Permanence of Paper for Printed Library Materials Z39.48-1984.

6   5   4   3   2   1

CONTENTS

PREFACE

In early 1985 The Johns Hopkins Foreign Policy Institute (FPI) of the School of Advanced International Studies (SAIS) was awarded support from the Carnegie Corporation of New York to engage in a twenty-four–month study of the implications of extraatmospheric technologies for U.S. foreign and defense policies. The study was chaired by Harold Brown, former secretary of defense and now the FPI chairman. It concentrated on the military implications of new technologies in space, including both support missions, such as communication and surveillance, and weapons aimed at satellites or at ballistic missiles. It took as its major premise the assumption that such space technologies are bound in some way to expand, limit, or define the options of future policymakers.

Throughout this program specific consideration was given to such questions as:

- Is "advantage" in space critical to future national security? How is advantage defined, and can technologies now under development credibly offer such advantage?

- What effects will various alternative policies for both developing and limiting the military uses of space have on the likelihood of nuclear war—or on its nature if it occurs?

- How is the traditional arms-control process applicable to space-based systems? Should arms-control objectives be limited from the outset? For example, can meaningful distinctions be made between antisatellite weapons (ASATs) and antiballistic missiles (ABMs)? Between low- and high-altitude ASATs? How do U.S.-Soviet negotiations on these matters relate to those on strategic or intermediate-range offensive nuclear forces?

- If space systems offer the potential for reinforcing national security, what share of the overall defense budget do they require? How should this allocation be divided among support systems and weapons?

- What will be the reaction of major allies to U.S. development of weapons in space, and to what extent can these allies be reassured in the light of their parochial interests?

- Is the military development of space divisible? In the presence of growing military technological capabilities and aspirations in space on both sides, how can a stable superpower balance in space be achieved?

To encourage a wide and open discussion on these questions, the FPI called upon a wide variety of experts, who met at SAIS on numerous occasions. These included a cross section of current government officials, members of Congress and their staff, former government officials, and experts from the national-security and scientific communities. We are enormously grateful for their help in the development of this study.

The essays that follow deal primarily with the impact of space technology on the foreign policy of the United States, including relations with the allies. Other SAIS Papers resulting from this program deal with such questions as the impact of such space technologies on the U.S. defense budget, their overall relevance to U.S. national security and arms control, and their consequences for U.S.-Soviet relations. All of these papers were written by SAIS faculty members and FPI associates.

We are especially grateful to the Carnegie Corporation of New York, which provided us with the support needed to undertake this program.

Simon Serfaty
Executive Director, FPI

INTRODUCTION

Before the nuclear age, war and preparation for war were the most conspicuous and, arguably, the dominant instruments of national power shaping international politics. Since the nuclear age began, war and preparation for war have been replaced by the arms race, deterrence, and arms control as the most conspicuous and the dominant instruments of power in international politics among the most powerful states.

With the emergence of the modern industrial-technological state and mass-based nationalism before the nuclear age, war and preparation for war increasingly preoccupied a professional elite and simultaneously engaged the ambitions and fears of national publics. With the infusion of nuclear technology into the armaments of the polarized postwar antagonists, the competitive pursuit of military strength, strategies of deterrence, and positions on arms control have reached a level of technical complexity and esoteric rationalization far exceeding the preoccupations of prenuclear elites. At the same time, the modalities of military confrontation and accommodation have affected and been affected by organized public sentiment to an extent unprecedented in history.

U.S. foreign policy and relations reflect this momentous magnification of the role of force in international politics. The peculiar intensity and complexity of the role of force short of war—whether through the medium of the arms race, deterrence strategy, or arms control—have exerted an especially pervasive influence on the United

States' relations with the Soviet Union and with its European allies. This phenomenon, however, has stimulated far less systematic and sophisticated inquiry into its political context than into its technical features. Given the relative susceptibility of technical complexities to at least the appearance of precise and elaborate reasoning, this is not surprising. But it can be dangerously misleading if it obscures the political implications of military developments.

This book, published by scholars of international politics and U.S. foreign and military policy at The Johns Hopkins School of Advanced International Studies (SAIS), is written to illuminate the political implications of what is the latest—surely not the last—and one of the most controversial military programs to seize the attention of national publics and elites since the H-bomb, *Sputnik*, and the antiballistic missile program: the Strategic Defense Initiative (SDI), announced by President Reagan on March 23, 1983. SDI is a striking manifestation of the enhanced role of military concerns in postwar U.S. foreign policy. No military program has had such a wide-ranging technological content. None has impinged so dramatically upon so many basic issues of arms competition, military strategy, and arms control. In governments and among defense and arms-control specialists SDI has ignited an explosion of technological assessments, strategic calculations, and arms-control prescriptions.

The authors of this study have not set out to reiterate these important inquiries and controversies. Instead, they have chosen to illuminate the larger context of East-West relations, U.S.-West European relations, and U.S. foreign and military policies in terms of which the political impact and implications of SDI must be explained. At the same time, they are aware of the extent to which such political considerations may be affected by technological and economic factors. Accordingly, they have taken these factors into account, as examined in other parts of the larger study undertaken by the Foreign Policy Institute, under the chairmanship of Harold Brown. Therefore, this book should be regarded, like all parts of the larger study, as an integral part of a comprehensive inquiry.

Robert E. Osgood
Christian A. Herter Professor
of American Foreign Policy, SAIS

1.
GENERAL CONSIDERATIONS ON SDI AND U.S. FOREIGN POLICY

Robert W. Tucker

In a recent essay on the technical prospects of the Strategic Defense Initiative, Britain's distinguished scientific adviser, Lord Zuckerman, observed: "Had anyone other than the American president ever invited scientists to try to render 'nuclear weapons impotent and obsolete', the suggestion would probably have attracted no more attention than had they been asked to square the circle or solve the problem of perpetual motion."[1] Zuckerman's point is by now a familiar one. To the many critics of the program, SDI exists because the president decreed that it exist. Leslie Gelb, reporting in *The New York Times* on the increasing momentum toward strategic defenses, declares that the "single most compelling reason for this is the force of Mr. Reagan's commitment and vision of transforming nuclear strategy from deterrence based on the threat of retaliation to peace based on effective defense. Administration skeptics say they dare not question this vision."[2]

There is evidently much to be said for this view. The president has not only been the prime but the indispensable mover of a program that must compete with other programs and that has drawn the opposition of many scientists and strategists. And it is only the president who is able, in the face of widespread opposition, to persuade a majority of the public that the vision he has evoked and the effort he has launched are deserving of support.

Even so, the emphasis regularly given to the role of the president may also prove misleading. It suggests that were it not for

Reagan's personal vision of a world free from the threat of nuclear missile weapons, a move toward defensive systems would never have arisen. But SDI is not simply the result of presidential fiat. It cannot be adequately explained without taking into account the sources of dissatisfaction and the unhappiness of a growing number with the nuclear strategy we have pursued since the 1960s. These sources have played an important role in the development of SDI. They also account, in part, for the public support given so far to SDI. The appeal of the program is varied and responds to fears and desires that are deep-rooted. It will not do, as many critics have done, to ignore these fears and desires or to treat them as somehow illegitimate. They not only tell us a good deal about the origins and present support of the Strategic Defense Initiative, they also throw light on the implications the program may have for the future.

THE IMPLICATIONS OF MUTUAL DETERRENCE

For a generation we have pursued a nuclear strategy of mutual deterrence through the threat of retaliation. At the time of its acceptance mutual deterrence was generally seen to reflect far more a necessity than a choice. Once accepted, efforts were directed to making mutual deterrence as safe and reliable as possible. How this might best be done gave rise to differences that remain unresolved today. The idea of mutual assured destruction provided one answer. Readily caricatured, if only by virtue of its acronym MAD, and clearly startling in its implications, it nevertheless expressed the prevailing view of the nuclear predicament, which was nothing other than the inordinate destructiveness of nuclear weapons and the apparent impossibility of mounting an effective defense against them. In these circumstances, the reasoning went, wisdom consisted in making a virtue of the nuclear vice by pursuing arrangements that would ensure that the use of nuclear weapons resulted in the common ruin of the attacked and the attacker. Given the prevailing inaccuracy of missiles, this meant a level of industrial and civilian destruction (cities) that would be unacceptable to either side. And given the state of defensive technology, it meant that efforts at defense would not only prove ineffective but destabilizing because of the fears and illusions they might encourage.

It is now largely forgotten that mutual deterrence through the threat (and presumably the certainty) of retaliation provided the answer for many who had taken a strong antinuclear position—indeed, who often had taken a position indistinguishable from nuclear pacifism. Yet the change from a position akin to nuclear pacifism to one strongly supporting deterrence was not so difficult to make. It followed, quite simply, from the conviction that mutual and assured destruction was the next best thing to the ideal—though impossible—solution. If we could not simply rid the world of nuclear weapons, then we could at least ensure that these weapons would never be used in view of the consequences to which their use must lead. To tamper in any way with this form of insurance must, it was thereafter argued, run the risk of leading us back to a world in which nuclear weapons might be used. It was not until the 1980s that a significant breach occurred in the ranks of the deterrence faithful, with many reverting in full or in part to a position they had earlier taken.

Mutual assured destruction was the latest version of the very old idea that war would disappear once its destructiveness promised to become sufficiently great. It was not the officials of the Kennedy and Johnson administrations who gave us this allegedly novel concept—as Reagan administration officials appear to believe—but a succession of eighteenth- to twentieth-century thinkers who were persuaded that advances in the technology of war must ultimately do away with war by making it too destructive. The same persuasion was voiced from the outset of the nuclear age. Indeed, the once most widely quoted expression of this theme came not from a visionary—or from a technocratic U.S. defense secretary—but from one of the century's greatest practitioners of statecraft, Winston Churchill, who remarked on the effect of nuclear weapons: "It may well be that we shall, by a process of sublime irony, have reached a stage in this story where safety will be the sturdy child of terror, and survival the twin brother of annihilation."

U.S. nuclear strategy continues to rest on the pervasive uncertainty attending any nuclear conflict between the superpowers. The various innovations in strategic doctrine since the early 1970s—from limited "nuclear options" through "countervailing" to "prevailing"—have not affected this uncertainty over whether meaningful limits can be placed on the use of nuclear weapons.

Nor has this uncertainty been affected significantly by the many refinements in nuclear weapons and, above all, by changes in their accuracy. The difference between the mutual assured destruction of a generation ago and the mutual deterrence of today is a difference of degree rather than kind. The vision of apocalypse has been slightly blurred, but it is still very much apparent.

The advent of mutual deterrence was a development of the first order of magnitude. It meant, quite simply, that the nation's historic security experience had come to a sudden and dramatic end. For the first time in our history, our physical existence had been put directly and completely to risk. The significance of this abrupt and wrenching change can scarcely be exaggerated. From the period of its infancy the United States had enjoyed an almost uniquely benign security experience, which was one of the great determinants in shaping the American character. It helped account for the optimism and sense of confidence with which, as a people, we have faced the future.

The two world wars had not brought this experience to an end, for the nation's physical security had not been directly threatened in either conflict. Although the United States had finally intervened in these wars, and particularly in World War II, out of balance-of-power considerations, an adverse outcome of either was not generally seen to threaten directly the country's core security. Instead, a fascist victory was seen to threaten the nation's greater-than-physical security, since it carried the prospect of a world in which the political and economic frontiers of the United States would have to become coterminous with its territorial frontiers, a world in which the American example and influence would become irrelevant.

But the Soviet acquisition of nuclear weapons and the means of their delivery did directly threaten, and with a vengeance, our physical security. Mutual deterrence was the U.S. government's response to this novel condition. Given formal sanction in the 1972 strategic arms agreements with the Soviet Union, mutual deterrence meant that this nation was now in the most literal sense a hostage to the power and intentions of the Soviet Union, just as the Soviet Union was a hostage to the power and intentions of the United States.

Nothing that has happened since World War II is comparable in significance to this change in U.S. security. Nothing has offset, or balanced, this change. Many intervening developments, of course, have profoundly altered the global power structure and, in consequence, U.S. security. The economic and political restoration of Western Europe and Japan and the breakup of what was once seen as a monolithic communist camp directed from Moscow are the most salient and notorious. These and other developments have, with few exceptions, worked to the advantage of the United States in its contest with the Soviet Union. But even if we take adequate account of the growing external and internal constraints on Soviet power, there remains the sea change in the U.S. position. Nothing, to repeat, quite compensates for this change.

The new strategic order of mutual deterrence through mutual vulnerability not only implied a radical change in the nation's security condition, it also implied a considerable change in our diplomatic tradition of unilateralism. This tradition, with its insistence upon complete independence of action, had always formed an essential part of the country's historic isolationism. Long seen as the virtual touchstone of an isolationist policy and outlook, unilateralism was not, in fact, abandoned during and immediately following World War II. The conventional view that it was abandoned, surviving only within the minority of right-wing isolationists, rests on a confusion of form with substance. Given the United States' vast power, the weakness of its major allies, and its continuing immunity from direct attack, an apparent devotion to multilateral forms in the postwar years masked the substance of what was largely unilateral action.

Mutual deterrence constituted a novel and significant constraint on what had previously been the scope of the nation's freedom of action. It did so if only by tying our fate to the fate of our great adversary, and in a way that was unprecedented. Even had the Soviet Union been a different type of state, this sudden involvement in a common fate represented a major change. Given the nature of the Soviet regime, given the fact that it represented the antithesis of what the United States stood for, and given our postwar aspirations to preside over an international order increasingly receptive to and reflective of American values and institutions, this mutual relationship should have been particularly difficult to accept.

Nor was the advent of mutual deterrence significant only for America's historic security position and its diplomatic tradition of unilateralism. The new nuclear strategy also carried important implications for the security of our major allies by measurably worsening the U.S. strategic predicament. The root of that predicament is found in the asymmetrical structure of interest that imposes more difficult and exacting deterrence requirements on the United States than on the Soviet Union. While the requirements for the Soviet Union extend no farther than Eastern Europe, for the United States they extend to Western Europe, Japan, and (possibly) the Persian Gulf. To a degree far greater than for the Soviet Union, deterrence for the United States has always been, and is today, an extension that includes others. By its very nature, extended deterrence must have much less credibility than self-deterrence. The liability of extended deterrence, moreover, cannot be fully compensated for by greater conventional forces. Greater conventional forces will raise the threshold of nuclear conflict, but they cannot preclude nuclear conflict. Ultimately, compensation must be found either at the strategic nuclear level or nowhere. It cannot be found at the strategic level by forces that are roughly equivalent to the Soviet Union and, especially, that are equally, if indeed not more, vulnerable. In these circumstances, the credibility of deterrence is bound to erode, the only question being how much.

STRATEGIC PARITY AND THE CHALLENGE TO EXTENDED DETERRENCE

In retrospect, it is remarkable how readily the nation adjusted to a strategy that carried these, and still other, adverse implications. In part, of course, the explanation lies in the widespread conviction that there was no real alternative to a nuclear strategy based on the mutual vulnerability of the United States and the Soviet Union. Mutual deterrence through the threat of retaliation was not seen as the result of theory or doctrine but of the nature of nuclear weapons and of technological prospects. Offensive weapons of ever-increasing accuracy and defensive systems based on exotic new technologies began to alter these prospects by the mid-to-late 1970s. But in the preceding decade, despite the interest in antiballistic missiles, the outlook appeared quite different. In the technological conditions of that period, mutual deterrence seemed far more a matter of necessity than of choice. The task of statesmanship, it was believed, was to recognize and to bow to this necessity, while directing one's efforts to making it as safe and reliable as possible. Moreover, it was assumed that in time the Soviet Union would also recognize and accept the condition of mutual vulnerability. The 1972 SALT I agreements were generally seen to validate this assumption.

These same years, roughly the decade following the Cuban missile crisis, were also marked by a significant change in outlook toward the political usefulness of nuclear weapons, a change that today is all too apparent. It finds frequent expression, particularly among those who were once high officials. One of them, a former secretary of defense, has recently declared: "Nuclear weapons serve no military purpose whatsoever. They are totally useless—except only to deter one's opponent from using them."[3] This revised attitude greatly eased the transition from a position of strategic superiority to one of rough equivalence characterizing mutual deterrence. For if it is accepted, very little—if, indeed, anything at all—is sacrificed in moving from a position of nuclear superiority to a position of nuclear parity. If strategic superiority is useless, in that it cannot be translated into diplomatic power or strategic advantage, then abandoning it must appear only reasonable.

What may be termed nuclear revisionism first appears as an influential view in the years following the Cuban missile crisis. Marking the end of the cold war, the Cuban missile crisis thereafter provided the prime illustration for those intent on demonstrating the political disutility of nuclear weapons. The marked disparity in nuclear forces, it has been argued, had no effect on the outcome of the crisis. Indeed, several of the members of the executive committee constituted to advise the president on the crisis have since testified that the possibility of using nuclear weapons was never considered. They have also noted that the disparity between the strategic forces of the two sides still could not have prevented the Soviet Union from imposing unprecedented destruction on this country, a prospect that by all accounts appalled president Kennedy. These considerations, however, do not disprove that the strategic superiority we enjoyed at the time had no effect on Soviet leadership and on the outcome of the crisis. They only show that it did not affect U.S. leadership in the sense that it did not prompt the Kennedy administration to attempt directly to exploit this superiority. To the contrary, president Kennedy and his associates explicitly refused to do so. There was no disposition, however, to refuse the indirect exploitation of strategic superiority. Such exploitation followed simply from the existence of a crisis in which the distinct possibility arose of the superpowers becoming directly engaged in a conventional military conflict.

The merit of nuclear revisionism apart, there is no question that the attitude it reflected aided the U.S. adjustment to the loss of strategic superiority. The Soviet achievement of strategic parity was an event of first-order importance, requiring a rethinking of the entire U.S. security position. Even if strategic superiority did not make extended deterrence *entirely* credible, it still made extended deterrence *more* credible, and it was on this credibility that the structure of American interests and commitments rested at the time and, in more difficult circumstances, continues to rest today. Strategic superiority made it much easier for the public to sustain a faith in U.S. ability to prevent nuclear war while protecting American vital interests. Yet, at the time, the effects of accepting a nuclear strategy of mutual vulnerability attracted only moderate attention and caused even less anxiety. In marked contrast to the early 1960s, the early 1970s gave rise to almost no agitation in the body politic over the nuclear issue, despite the momentous changes that had occurred.

It is in the prevailing political circumstances of the time that one finds the principal reason for the absence of much concern over the long-term consequences of mutual deterrence. There was, of course, the war in Vietnam and the almost obsessive preoccupation of government, elites, and public with the war. Vietnam aside, the reason for the relative lack of concern over the extraordinary change that was taking place was because we were in the floodtide of détente. Having developed slowly and unevenly in the course of the 1960s, by the early 1970s, détente had become the centerpiece of the Nixon policy reformulation. In the context of détente, the loss of strategic superiority was seen by some as an event without great significance and by others as an event that, although regrettable, could be taken in stride. Instead, greater attention was directed to SALT I, although the tangible results of the talks were almost inconsequential compared with the Soviet Union's achievement of strategic parity. But the arms-control negotiations were considered almost from the outset a litmus test of the overall relationship of the superpowers. If this relationship was relatively good, it was assumed, the possible consequences of the new strategic dispensation afforded little ground for concern.

The relative equanimity that marked the transition of the world of strategic parity provides eloquent testimony to the primacy of politics in nuclear matters. It demonstrates vividly that what is ultimately at issue in the persisting debate over nuclear weapons and strategy are not technical considerations but varying judgments about the character and aspirations of the Soviet regime. In this debate, how the opposing sides interpret the necessary and sufficient conditions of deterrence depends in large measure on what they believe about the nature of the U.S.-Soviet conflict. For most of the decade leading up to the 1972 SALT I agreements, the predominant view of this conflict was one of rising optimism. This accounts for the relative ease with which the nation adjusted to a nuclear strategy based on the mutual vulnerability of the United States and the Soviet Union. And more than any other factor, this accounts for the continuing credibility of extended deterrence.

The hopes and expectations placed in détente were not realized. By the middle of the 1970s, détente was giving way; by the end of the decade, it had collapsed. During these same years the belief grew that the Soviet government had not accepted the U.S. view of mutual deterrence but was engaged instead in a serious and sustained effort to overcome its own vulnerability. In these circumstances anxiety over the credibility of extended deterrence steadily increased. Evidence of this is found in the evolution of American strategic doctrine. Since the early 1970s strategic doctrines have increasingly assumed the function of bridging the apparently growing gap between the forces needed for a credible extended deterrence and the forces in being. If the gap could no longer be satisfactorily bridged in fact, it could still be bridged in word. Without ever claiming strategic superiority—indeed, even while expressly disavowing an interest in seeking superiority—the United States has attempted to salvage at least some residual benefits of superiority. Thus the claim of the Carter administration that we could still ensure that the Soviets would always lose more than they would gain from resorting to any kind of armed aggression (''countervailing'').

Or the more pretentious claim of the Reagan administration that in a nuclear conflict our forces would have the capability of imposing an early termination of the conflict on terms favorable to this country ("prevailing").

THE RISE OF THE ANTINUCLEAR MOVEMENT

With the coming to office of Ronald Reagan, the nation had for the first time a president and an administration whose hostility to the nuclear strategy of the 1960s and 1970s was deep-seated and well advertised. Yet it was not the Reagan administration that mounted the first great assault on mutual deterrence but the antinuclear movement that suddenly arose during Reagan's first year in office. The antinuclear movement, which dominated the scene from 1981 to 1984, was unprecedented both for the abruptness with which it arose and for the breadth of support it appeared to enjoy. As late as the winter of 1979–80, there was little to indicate that nuclear weapons would become the critical issue of public discourse they did become by the fall of 1981. And whereas the antinuclear movements of the past (particularly the early 1960s) represented little more than the stirring of a few, the movement of the 1980s assumed mass proportions. Not only was the later movement far stronger than its predecessors, its effect on the Reagan administration was far greater.

At the outset the Reagan administration set its face against the peace movement and rejected its principal demand of a freeze on the deployment, testing, and manufacture of nuclear weapons. But despite an initial insensitivity and resistance to public anxiety on the nuclear issue, after scarcely a year in office the administration began, slowly but surely, to respond to public concern. The occasional lapses in discussing the use of weapons, lapses that many found so alarming, stopped. More significantly, the virtually dismissive attitude toward arms control changed, and if the change was scarcely in the nature of a conversion, it was nonetheless a change both in rhetoric and even in policy. Finally, and perhaps most significantly, the administration came forth in March 1983 with its real response to the anxiety and dissatisfaction reflected by the antinuclear movement—the Strategic Defense Initiative.

At the time, and even now, the prevailing view of the anti-nuclear movement finds its origins in the statements and, even more, the outlook of the Reagan administration. But the lapse of faith in deterrence, which was the most important characteristic of the movement, is largely trivialized by this explanation. The initial behavior of the Reagan administration may be regarded as triggering the antinuclear movement; it cannot be plausibly seen as the deeper cause of this movement and the lapse of faith it represented. For this, we must look primarily to the decline and fall of détente. While it lasted, faith in deterrence went largely unquestioned. It did so despite the fact that many of the developments that so alarmed the peace movement in the 1980s were apparent enough in the mid-to-late 1970s. But so long as a semblance of détente remained, anxiety over the "arms race" and the dangers it presumably holds, as well as alarm over the political and moral hazards of the present structure of deterrence, were apparently held to modest levels. It is in the fall of détente and the rise of a new cold war that we must find the simple but critical explanation for the antinuclear arms movement.

At the same time the deeper implications of this movement may, and very likely do, have an enduring significance. Thus, the faith once generally held in mutual deterrence seems unlikely to be restored. This is plausible, even without taking into account the impact of the Reagan administration's Strategic Defense Initiative and the justification given on its behalf, although the effect of both is to deal a further blow to what was once a quite robust faith.

A decline of faith in the effectiveness of the deterrent structure of the past generation has been accompanied by an erosion in our moral judgment of that structure. The extent of this change is indicated by comparing the position taken in 1965 by Vatican Council II with the position taken in 1983 by American Catholic bishops.[4] A generation ago the Vatican Council pointedly refrained from condemning a structure of deterrence that rested, in the last resort, upon the threat of indiscriminate warfare. While warning that deterrence was "not a safe way to preserve a steady peace," the council nevertheless approved of deterrence. Nor did it condemn nuclear war. What it condemned, and all that it condemned, was "total war" and any acts of war "aimed indiscriminately at the destruction of entire cities or extensive areas along with their population."

By contrast, the American bishops condemn virtually any and every possible form of nuclear war. The use of nuclear weapons is rejected, whether they are used against military targets or against civilian centers of population, whether in a first strike or a retaliatory second strike, whether in a central or in a theater nuclear war. The bishops take this position because they are convinced nuclear weapons cannot be controlled or their effects limited. On the other hand, Vatican Council II limited itself to a careful statement of the circumstances in which the use of nuclear weapons must be condemned.

The moral condemnation of nuclear war—any and every nuclear war—is a position that is generally shared by the deterrence faithful. But for those who believe strongly enough in the effectiveness of mutual deterrence, the immorality of nuclear war need not present a considerable problem. Even if the price for holding an evil intent is the moral deformation of the holder, it makes a great difference whether one believes that while the prospects of doing evil are nearly nonexistent, the consequences of not threatening to do evil are very real. The matter is otherwise, however, for those who do not entertain a strong belief in the effectiveness of mutual deterrence or have experienced a lapse of faith. Once mutual deterrence is deprived of its saving grace—the promise that it will never have to be put to use—it must give rise to a growing sense of despair, moral and otherwise.

The American bishops' letter points in this direction as do similar recent pronouncements on the illegitimacy of ever using nuclear weapons. Although the "strictly conditioned moral acceptance" it gives to deterrence contrasts with its almost flat rejection of the use of nuclear weapons, the meaning of the apparent contrast depends on the optimism with which deterrent structures are viewed. Once the confidence formerly invested in them declines, as it has today, the illegitimacy with which the use—any use—of nuclear weapons is increasingly viewed will characterize the moral judgment made of mutual deterrence.

SDI AND THE NATURE OF DETERRENCE

The peace movement of the early 1980s helped to create an environment receptive to the Reagan administration's Strategic

Defense Initiative. It did so by its attack on mutual deterrence. To be sure, the motives of those who led the antinuclear movement differed markedly from the motives of those supporting the president's program. Even so, this consideration may be less important than the fact that both the peace movement and the administration's supporters have contributed to the same general result. Moreover, in one decisive respect there is clearly an essential similarity in motivation. Whatever the other differences separating a Jonathan Schell from Ronald Reagan, both have been motivated by a deep unhappiness with and grave apprehension over the structure of deterrence we have lived with for the past generation. For both, the escape from a world in which it is "necessary to rely on the specter of retaliation," to use the president's words, is not deemed only desirable but necessary. Time alone, Schell has urged, must transform the possibility of nuclear war into a probability. The crisis in deterrence stems, at bottom, from nothing more than the "continuing reliance on nuclear arms."[5] Schell's view is only a step removed from the president's conviction that it is "inconceivable...that we can go on thinking down the future, not only for ourselves and for our lifetimes, but for other generations, that the great nations of the world will sit here, like people facing themselves across a table, each with a cocked gun, and no one knowing whether someone might tighten their finger on the trigger."[6]

The president's aversion to the present system of deterrence should have come as no surprise. He had expressed hostility to mutual deterrence on many occasions during the preceding decade. Reagan's views were, by and large, similar to those generally entertained on the political Right. For many years the Right had expressed skepticism over mutual deterrence, attacking it not only on strategic grounds but on political and moral grounds as well. Time and intervening developments served to sharpen this criticism. Although the essential critique of mutual deterrence remained substantially unchanged from the early 1970s to the mid-1980s, its persuasiveness did change. Intervening developments—technological, strategic, and political—did appear to lend greater persuasiveness to the critique, while placing supporters of mutual deterrence increasingly on the defensive. Technological developments alone had this effect. The advent of offensive missile systems of greater accuracy and the prospect of missile defenses combined to call into greater question than ever before the condition of mutual vulnerability.

It also became increasingly apparent that the Soviet leadership never really shared American acceptance of this condition. Instead, from the outset it pursued a strategy designed to limit the Soviet Union's vulnerability by developing a strategic force with the capability of attacking the U.S. land-based missile system. The Soviet pursuit of a first-strike capability (or, if one prefers, of a damage limitation capability) has prompted the conclusion by critics of mutual deterrence that a ''stable relationship of mutual deterrence'' has never existed.[7] The conclusion goes much too far. It equates the fact, or condition, of stability based on mutual deterrence with the effort to upset this condition. Even so, save for those who believe that deterrence is not only an inherent property of nuclear missile weapons but very nearly a self-sufficient property, the Soviet strategic effort since the early 1970s has served to strengthen the Right's case against the present system of deterrence.

This case, it needs to be emphasized, goes well beyond the vagaries of technological development and the vicissitudes of Soviet strategic programs. In its broader dimensions it rests on the contention that the strategic order of deterrence based on mutual vulnerability is flawed at its very core. For that order presumably incorporates two incompatible elements that, like oil and water, will always separate. Fred Ikle puts the matter thus:

> [T]he accord on a stable equilibrium of mutual restraint is psychologically incompatible with the constant threat of reciprocal annihilation. The first ingredient of this mixture represents the best in international relations: a continued willingness to cooperate in restraining one's own military power, coupled with a serene reliance on the opponent's prudence and his common sense. The second ingredient of the mixture represents the worst in international relations: an endless effort to maintain forces that are constantly ready to annihilate the opponent, coupled with an unremitting determination to deny him escape from this grip of terror.[8]

The believers in a viable, that is, a stable system of mutual deterrence based on mutual vulnerability, Ikle argues, fail to appreciate the dynamic of this incompatibility. They do not see the essential instability of this order with its ceaseless tilting and its never-ending adjustments of a quivering balance. But if this order is essentially unstable—a judgment the record does not yet vindicate—it is so primarily for other reasons. Ikle's incompatible ingredients are essentially the same ingredients that have made up most international orders we have known. His criticism of the order based on mutual deterrence is more properly a criticism of the paradox that characterizes international order as such, and that does so of necessity. Every international order rests on a "willingness to cooperate in restraining one's own military power" as well as a reliance, though not necessarily a "serene reliance," on the opponent's prudence. At the same time, every international order rests on the threat of punishment if the tacit "social contract" is broken. If the order of mutual deterrence holds the threat of annihilation, as Ikle notes, this results more from the nature of the weapons on which this order rests than from the particular strategic disposition of these weapons. It is true that the order of mutual deterrence pushes this conventional wisdom respecting the basis of international order to its *reductio ad absurdum*. But this, again, is less the result of the doctrine of consensual vulnerability than of the character of the weapons themselves.

If the present order of mutual deterrence is inherently flawed, as Ikle and others believe, this results less from the principles on which the order of deterrence is based than from the parties that compose it. The oil and water, it turns out, are the United States and the Soviet Union. If the mutuality required of deterrence can lead only to disaster, this is because it must be entered into with a state like the Soviet Union. This has always been the essential point in the Right's critique of mutual deterrence. What is seen as the failure of mutual deterrence and of concomitant efforts at arms control are not primarily the result either of conceptual error or of technical misjudgment—though these played a role—but of political misjudgment. Mutual deterrence, along with the arms-control measures undertaken to strengthen it, depended centrally on a certain assessment of the party with whom we would undertake this relationship. This assessment was badly in error, in this view, because of the nature of the Soviet regime and, to a lesser although still important degree, because of the nature of democratic societies.

Ultimately, this is the crucial reason why, according to the conservative critique, the present system of mutual deterrence holds for us a peril that can only grow. The Western democracies, Ikle has written, "will have to defend themselves for the foreseeable future against the military might and political ambition of the Soviet ruling class, still dominated by men imbued with Lenin's totalitarian philosophy." Ikle eschews speculation on the ways by which the threat of nuclear destruction may be turned into the "ideal instrument for totalitarian expansion." But he is confident that the " 'balance of terror' cannot favor the defense of a democratic alliance. Sooner or later it will favor those most at ease with, those most experienced in, the systematic use of terror." Moreover, a continued reliance on the present system of mutual deterrence foreordains the West's demoralization, a condition that will result simply from the vision of a future in which we are resigned to "the possibility of an atrocity unsurpassed in human history."[9]

The promise of the Strategic Defense Initiative is to redress this pervasive pessimism by holding out the prospect of escaping its consequences. Technology, and technological optimism, will presumably provide the answer to politics, and political pessimism. In the short term, supporters of the initiative promise, technology can deliver us from the immediate perils of vulnerability by strengthening a now defective system of deterrence and through a point defense of missile sites. In the longer run, the promise is held out of fashioning an effective defense against ballistic missiles. Such a world will still fall far short of the president's vision of a world in which nuclear weapons are rendered impotent and thus no longer play a role, for this world would require denying the strategic use of not only space, and therefore of ballistic missiles, but of air space as well, and therefore of air-breathing conveyances. A defense against ballistic missiles would still leave us in a world of nuclear weapons. Moreover, it would leave us in a world of mutual deterrence through the threat of retaliation. It may well be, as Ikle has argued, that this would represent a great gain for the following reasons:

> Bombers and cruise missiles, compared with ballistic missiles, are less suited for surprise attack because of their longer time of travel. And bombers are safer as deterrent forces since, by

taking to the air, they can be made nearly invulnerable to an alert, yet could safely return to their bases should the warning be false. Also, using in part the same technologies and systems, air defense could later complement our ballistic missile defenses.[10]

Even if these reasons are at once accepted, a world in which ballistic missiles played a diminishing role would still be a world of mutual deterrence. The U.S.-Soviet strategic relationship would still be characterized by mutual vulnerability and might be more stable than it is today for the reasons Ikle advances. People's anxieties might be lessened and their hopes strengthened. But these considerations do not affect the point that essentially the present system of mutual vulnerability will have been improved. It will still be mutual and, one is forced to add, it will still be just as much—or as little—"consensual" as it is today.

Altogether different, of course, is a world in which Reagan's grand vision is realized and nuclear weapons are rendered impotent altogether. The promise of transcending the age of deterrence makes up the political appeal of SDI. The world this vision encompasses is not one in which faith in deterrence is somehow restored by altering the technical arrangements on which this system rests, but one in which there is no longer a need to restore faith. In this world the deterrence of today, and possibly of tomorrow, will be replaced by a new relationship. This relationship, if we are to credit the president and supporters of his vision, will differ profoundly from the present one. Whereas the current relationship is constituted by a sword—a devastating sword—without a shield, the new one presumably will be constituted by a shield without a sword. The mutual deterrence of yesterday and today threaten an opponent with terrible retaliation should he resort to aggression. The deterrence of tomorrow and the day after tomorrow must rest on the same threat, for the movement from ballistic missiles to bombers and cruise missiles would signal no change in this respect. But in the world of President Reagan's sweeping vision, the greater aggressor might well be visited with no punishment at all. "Our goal," Secretary Weinberger has stated, "is to destroy weapons that kill people."[11] The other and better means of deterring war, Reagan has said of his defense initiative is "by means other than threatening devastation to any aggressor—and by a means which threatens no one."[12]

The contention that this "new" deterrence will destroy weapons rather than people forms the basis of its claim to a higher morality. If ever realized, the claim would certainly prove justified. Although the deterrent arrangement under which we presently live differs in critical respects from the deterrence known in ages past, it does at least preserve this continuity with the past: it rests on a social principle, reciprocity, which has nearly always been the most reliable in setting restraints on man's collective behavior. It differs from the past by not carrying but threatening to carry this principle to an extreme limit. But the deterrence under which we will presumably live one day has no apparent continuity with the past. While holding out the "threat" of disarming an aggressor, it does so for no ostensible purpose other than defense. The destruction of an aggressor's weapons is not a step preparatory to the imposition of one's will, let alone the wreaking of vengeance. Instead, it is presented as an end in itself, and this despite the fact that it will have been taken to ward off an annihilating act of aggression. In the history of state relations, this idea of saving all lives rather than avenging some lives would surely represent, if ever acted upon, something new under the sun.

THE APPEAL OF SDI

The issue of motivation may be briefly considered against this general background. In regard to the prime movers of the defense initiative, there is little to add to accounts already available.[13] The story of how President Reagan came to embrace the idea of strategic defense and to make it one of the great projects of his administration has been told many times. His antipathy to the present system of deterrence goes back many years and was expressed in the presidential campaigns of 1976 and 1980. Mutual deterrence based on the threat of destruction has been likened by Mr. Reagan to two men holding cocked pistols to each other's heads. Aside from eliciting his strong moral disapproval, mutual deterrence is condemned because it holds out a future devoid of hope. Ikle's description of this expected future—"a prospect of anxiety without relief, an intellectual legacy crippling the outlook of each new generation, a theme of desolate sadness"[14]—is a more elegant statement of the president's view and explains his conviction that "there must be another way."

Moreover, the appeal of SDI is not only that it is another way but that it has particular appeal to the president and to those who share his outlook. If the true believers in SDI, beginning with the president, are technological optimists, it is partly because they are political pessimists. At bottom, they entertain little expectation that we will ever achieve a political relationship with the Soviet Union that finds expression in a more satisfactory strategic military relationship. Given this outlook, the only prospect for changing an unsatisfactory and even dangerous strategic relationship, while not surrendering vital political interests, is of necessity technological. It has special appeal, not only because it relies on exploiting our vaunted technological superiority, but because it can be pursued independently of the will or desire of the Soviet Union or, for that matter, of allies. SDI suggests to many the recapture of an independence of action, which was lost with the onset of the period of mutual deterrence.

If these were the general considerations that marshaled the president's advocacy of SDI, there were other more specific, and pressing, considerations that affected decisionmakers. SDI was undertaken at a time when the antinuclear movement enjoyed considerable momentum. At the very least, the movement indicated an erosion in the support that deterrent arrangements had formerly enjoyed. More than this, the movement suggested to many within the Reagan administration the beginning of a trend that might end by challenging in toto the legitimacy of mutual deterrence. Certainly, a number of signs—the Catholic bishops' letter being the most notorious—pointed in that direction.

While the antinuclear (freeze) movement had not deterred the Reagan adminstration from undertaking a strategic force modernization program, it did make it more difficult to line up congressional and public support for the program. This was apparent in the case of the MX missile. Clearly, the administration had only itself to blame for a large part of the difficulty it had with Congress over the MX when it betrayed an inadvertence that was impressive by almost any standard. Even so, a part of the administration's difficulties with Congress over the MX would very likely have arisen regardless of its behavior. The not unreasonable conviction grew that the apparent fate of the MX might well be the fate of any land-based missile system proposed in the future. And if this should prove to be the case, it was increasingly asked, what might happen to the U.S. land-based deterrent, if the Soviets continued unchecked their efforts in offensive land missiles?

In some measure, then, the defense initiative responded to apprehensions over what was seen as a growing domestic challenge to the order of mutual deterrence. SDI was to be the instrument for creating a new political consensus in place of the former one, which was now plainly eroding. An emphasis on defense, on destroying weapons rather than killing people, would appeal across the political spectrum. So too, it was and is believed, the prospect of a world ultimately free of the threat of nuclear weapons would appeal to those in the peace movement who had increasingly lost faith in mutual deterrence.

To these attractions of SDI must be added the quite different appeal the program holds for many whose interests are of a different order. Those within the administration who were initially surprised by, and even opposed to, the president's initiative, soon showed a remarkable degree of support. One explanation, of course, is that faith in SDI—or at least the appearance of faith—at once became the litmus test of loyalty to the president. Yet another explanation is simply that SDI began to appeal considerably to those persuaded that the nation's strategic position was constantly eroding. From this perspective SDI could be supported if only as a measure of insurance against the danger of being surprised by Soviet developments in missile defense (and, more generally, as a program to deepen our own understanding of the prospects for missile defense).

This purely precautionary rationale for SDI, however, scarcely accounts for the impressive early momentum of the program and the bureaucratic support it has elicited even among many who were initially skeptical of it. In part, the enthusiasm among the once-reserved lies in the promise SDI is seen to hold out as a solution to the predicament of extended deterrence. Strategic defense is expected to restore the cohesiveness of our major alliance by restoring the credibility of extended deterrence. It will presumably do so, however, without attempting to recapture strategic superiority. Indeed, from the outset administration officials have emphatically disavowed strategic superiority as a goal of the U.S. defense effort.

Is this denial to be taken at face value? It is not easy to do so. The contention that SDI will largely restore the credibility of extended deterrence follows from the claim that it will, at the very least, enhance mutual deterrence by markedly improving the prospect that a substantial portion of the U.S. land-based intercontinental ballistic missile (ICBM) force will survive a first strike. This prospect, moreover, is expected to materialize in the early stages of the defense transition, since it will result largely from the effective defense of missile sites. Thus, the technologically easiest and economically cheapest part of the defense initiative will soon relieve us of much of the anxiety we presently experience.

The strengthening of mutual deterrence, however, is not the same thing as the restoration of a credible extended deterrence. Clearly, stable mutual deterrence forms the essential precondition of all else. Even so, it will not be sufficient to restore the credibility extended deterrence once enjoyed, or was believed to have enjoyed. Indeed, critics of the present system have long contended that what is required for the credible deterrence of an attack on this country must be sharply distinguished from what is required for the credible deterrence of others. The requirements of extended deterrence, they have argued, are much more onerous and exacting, and this is particularly so for a strategy of extended deterrence that continues to rest on the threat to use nuclear weapons first in response to a Soviet conventional attack on our European allies. The unwillingness to confront squarely this growing predicament of extended deterrence and to take the needed measures, critics have contended, has become a major cause of today's strategic instability. "The absence of war probably reflects," one critic has recently written, "the fact that nuclear deterrence has not undergone the severe test of an acute military crisis in over two decades. There is now little basis for confidently assuming that deterrence stability will survive the next acute military crisis—whenever it may occur."[15]

From the perspective of those who have always emphasized the exacting requirements of extended deterrence and have persistently stressed the inadequacy of meeting these requirements by a strategy of mutual assured destruction, SDI is attractive because it holds the promise of restoring at least some semblance of strategic superiority. And from this perspective the disclaimers that "the United States patently has no plans to restore its former advantage in global nuclear arms''[16] are difficult to credit. Particularly when considered together with present programs for developing offensive counterforce weapons, SDI must appear as part of an overall effort to recapture what the United States lost a generation ago. Certainly, to the Soviet Union, the pursuit of counter-silo weapons and of strategic defenses must be, and is, seen as an attempt by the United States to regain a credible first-strike capability, thereby altering substantially, if not eliminating, the vulnerability to Soviet nuclear attack we have experienced since the early 1960s.

SDI AND THE PROSPECTS FOR PEACE

Any speculation on the general implications of SDI for the future of U.S. foreign policy must begin by making certain assumptions, particularly about technological prospects, which remain very much at issue today. Of almost equal importance to technological considerations are the pace at which and the determination with which the two sides proceed with their respective efforts. Then, too, the impact of SDI on the U.S.-Soviet relationship cannot be considered in isolation from the general geopolitical setting. Much will depend on the state of the overall political relationship between the two states in the years during which the defense initiative proceeds.

At one extreme, we may assume that successive administrations proceed apace with SDI, that the effort enjoys strong public support, that it is marked by striking technological successes, that the several stages of the defensive transition are accordingly telescoped, that the Soviet Union fails to match U.S. efforts (whether in devising countermeasures or in developing comparable defensive systems of its own) and falls steadily behind in the competition, and that the general geopolitical environment is no better than it is today and, what is more likely, is somewhat worse. In these circumstances, it seems reasonable to assume, the arms-control process must either break down altogether or, even if continued, become devoid of any meaning.

On the basis of these assumptions, an alarming scenario may be drawn. The Soviets find their strategic position steadily eroding. A mounting anxiety over this development is in no way assuaged by the geopolitical environment. Whether they look to the West, the East, or the South, political trends point to increasing difficulties in maintaining their present position, let alone in improving it. Rather than remaining passive in the face of these developments, it has been argued that Moscow may feel driven to launch an attack on some central component of our as yet unprotected strategic defenses, which—though falling short of a first strike against the U.S. retaliatory capability—would still represent an act of war, with all its attendant dangers. It would do so for the same reasons that great powers in the past have struck out once they have concluded that they are being increasingly pressed on all sides and that time is working to their disadvantage.

From this perspective, SDI raises the prospect of precipitating a war—and perhaps a nuclear war—between the superpowers. Nor is it necessary, in this view, to add unfavorable political developments to what the Soviet leadership is already likely to see as sufficient reason for taking extreme measures, that is, the unilateral deployment by the United States of an increasingly effective defense against ballistic missiles. The Reagan administration understandably has soft-pedaled this contingency either by ignoring the prospect altogether or by assuming the "parallel deployment" of defensive systems. What if this assumption is not borne out and the other side begins to lag considerably behind? The prospect that it will do so was, after all, the expectation and hope of many who initially pushed for the defense initiative. U.S. technological superiority, it was urged, would enable us to make an end run around the Soviets. But in that event, Moscow would be confronted with the prospect of unilateral deployment that has so frightened the Reagan administration. If the Soviet Union deployed such systems unilaterally, administration officials have contended, deterrence would collapse and, according to a White House pamphlet, "We would have no choices between surrender and suicide."[17] It would not be surprising if Soviet officials took a similar view of their prospects in contemplating U.S. unilateral deployment of an effective defense.

The view outlined above ought not to be confused with the position that SDI is dangerous because it will intensify or heighten the risks of the dynamic of the arms race. The position that SDI will increase the pressure on both sides to use their nuclear weapons in a crisis, if only because defensive systems will dramatically reduce already short reaction times, finds the danger primarily in the technology itself, or rather in man's inability to control the technology. The fear is not the result of technology as such. Instead, it is the age-old fear of falling behind and losing one's place. The great danger of SDI does not result from technological determinism but from the Soviet fear that they will lose, or are losing, their hard-earned position of strategic parity with all that this loss entails.

The evident strength of this view is its appeal to history. Our experience with great-power conflicts does appear to support the position that in circumstances roughly comparable to those sketched out above, great powers have often gone to war. Is it plausible, though, to assume these circumstances in the present case? Does the history of the arms competition between the United States and the Soviet Union support the assumption of a critical U.S. technological triumph that goes unmatched—or uncompensated—by the Soviet Union? Certainly, this particular arms competition, now stretching over almost four decades, does not appear to bear it out. What it does point to is the ability of the more technologically backward of the two states either to match the strides of its adversary or to devise compensatory measures. It is true that we are told that this time will be different because the technological race is more difficult than ever and the Soviets are less prepared than ever to run it. But we have been told the same before, and we have been startled more than once to find that the adversary has not only run the race but finished in good time.

The critical assumption of a great disparity between the results of the respective efforts of the two sides is one that the history of the past forty years does not appear to support. Yet, it does support the assumption that a modest disparity may arise and has arisen without resulting in dangerous instability. Of course, it may be argued that the past is largely irrelevant to the present and future because the position of the Soviet Union has now fundamentally changed. In the past the Soviet Union was bent on establishing strategic equality with the United States. As the contender, it had to accept, and could afford to accept, disparities that it will find incompatible with its status as a strategic coequal.

This argument—as well as the larger view of which it is a part—does not share the belief that nuclear weapons have fundamentally altered the outlook and calculations of great powers and, particularly, the interests over which great powers have been willing in the past to go to war with other great powers. If this is indeed the case, then the implications of the defense initiative may well be as somber as they are often depicted by critics. For even if it is accepted that the circumstances corresponding to those assumptions earlier summarized are not likely to arise, they may do so. And if they do, the one remaining barrier to a catastrophic conflict is precisely the barrier posed by nuclear weapons themselves, a barrier that is largely brushed aside, however, by assimilating the conflicts between great nuclear powers to the conflicts between great powers in the past.

What must be questioned, though, is precisely this assumption of a continuity with the past. Admittedly, the appeal to experience is limited. Still, the view that nuclear weapons have effected a basic change in the nature of great-power conflicts rests on something more solid than intuition. During the past generation a common persuasion has grown that, short of surrender, no outcome of a crisis, however grave, could be worse than initiating a nuclear war. This persuasion is novel. Its effect is to confine the prospects of war between the great nuclear powers within limits that are far narrower than they have ever been. The significance of this persuasion is that it makes the risk of nuclear war virtually synonymous with the danger of miscalculation. It is the risk of miscalculation in severe crises that now defines the residual risk of nuclear war.

Nor is this all. While it may be said that many wars resulted from miscalculation, this consideration is almost irrelevant today because a war between nuclear superpowers would be one of miscalculation in a sense heretofore unknown. Given its expected speed and destructiveness, a nuclear war enables us to see the future as we have never before been able to see it. The calculations, and miscalculations, that once extended over months and years now extend over hours and days. The uncertainties that formerly attended the decision for war, and did so as late as World War II, have been replaced by the near certainties attending nuclear war between the superpowers. What does remain uncertain is not the minimum extent of destruction each side would suffer, but whether this destruction would permit the continuity and cohesiveness of national life in its wake. This is not the question national leaders literally asked themselves in 1914 or, for that matter, in 1939. And even if they had, they were not confronted with the direct and brutal answer nuclear weapons present.

Seeing the future as they have never before been permitted to see it, governments—the Soviet government included—may be expected to resist accepting it more determinedly than ever before. Even so, a risk of miscalculation will remain so long as the possibility exists that in a severe crisis the moment may come when circumstances conspire to make nuclear war appear inevitable. Logically, that time should never come. If no outcome of a crisis, short of outright surrender, could be worse for either side than the outcome represented by nuclear war, neither side should ever be tempted to miscalculate. The danger, we know, is that this logic will break down in a severe crisis and that one side or both sides will become increasingly persuaded of the inevitability of nuclear war.

Once that persuasion takes hold, a very different logic becomes operative. If nuclear war is once considered inevitable, striking first may be a considerable advantage, even in the absence of defensive systems. At any rate, the temptation to believe in such advantage may prove irresistible, and particularly so once even a limited defense system is in place. Even a terminal defense system must encourage the expectation (and, on the other side, the fear) that by striking first, the adversary's remaining forces may be sufficiently depleted to be employed effectively in a counterforce strategy. In these circumstances the side that has been struck first may well face the painful choice between escalating the exchange or accepting defeat. This is, of course, the same choice that those alarmed over the Soviet land-based missile buildup have long emphasized. The "window of vulnerability" to which this buildup has supposedly led is to be overcome, however, by creating another window of vulnerability, one that is likely to represent an even greater danger.

Still, these considerations do not essentially affect the point that the conclusion of inevitability is the decisive factor. At most, they suggest that the definition or scope of inevitability must be slightly broadened. But the view that assimilates the conflicts between the great nuclear powers to past great-power conflicts does not, need not, make the contingency of nuclear war dependent on the conclusion of inevitability that could emerge in a severe crisis. Nor does it consider that this conclusion is of necessity a miscalculation in the sense that if each party has sufficient information about the other party's intentions, there would be no nuclear war. Instead, it finds the calculations leading to nuclear war to differ little from the calculations that led to war in the past. The conclusion of inevitability that is decisive in its calculations is one that emerges outside the context of a severe crisis because it no longer has the quality of immediacy.

If this view is accepted, we live in a more dangerous world than even most pessimists have imagined. If nuclear weapons have not essentially altered the motivations and calculations that led great powers to war in the past, the avoidance of nuclear conflict in the future will require more than simply the abandonment of SDI. Instead, such avoidance may well depend upon holding out to the Soviet Union the assurance that the present strategic relationship will not be altered in any significant manner by this country.

SDI AND THE PROSPECTS FOR AN ARMS AGREEMENT

A quite different view of the future from the foregoing follows from the assumptions that beyond terminal defense, the U.S. effort will prove no more than moderately successful, that this effort will extend over a generation, that the Soviets will compensate for U.S. efforts in part by their own more modest progress and in part through taking effective countermeasures, and that the political climate marginally improves in comparison to the past five years. While these assumptions may turn out to have been mistaken, from the present perspective they seem reasonable. A defense effort that is moderately successful may be considered as one comprising both endo- and exo-atmospheric elements and capable of destroying one-half to three-quarters of warheads in a Soviet first strike. This may fall well below the expectations of SDI enthusiasts, but it would nevertheless represent a considerable technological achievement and one that many experts continue to doubt. Whether it would give this country a "damage limiting" capability remains doubtful if only given the prospect of Soviet proliferation in order to keep the same target coverage.

If these assumptions about the future are granted, what are their implications for U.S. foreign policy? What changes might follow from them? I would argue that very little may be expected to change—at least, very little that would not have changed for other reasons. This conclusion is at variance with the view that an increasing U.S. commitment to defensive systems will, if persisted in, largely destroy any remaining prospects for further arms-control agreements. One response to this is that the prospects for arms control do not appear very bright in any event, despite the apparent centrality the issue now has in the U.S.-Soviet relationship. Any future major arms-control agreement must be negotiated against the background of an experience that will make further agreements very difficult to reach. This experience is regarded as one tantamount to betrayal by a critically important political constituency. Having found our security interests weakened by the arms-control agreements of the 1970s and having been persuaded that Moscow will enter into a pact with this country only when it can gain political advantage from doing so, the Right's disposition (or inclination) to resist further agreements will be quite strong. It is not at all clear that this resistance could be overcome.

In any case, the prospects—such as they are—for a major agreement on strategic weapons are likely to decline with the passage of time, especially if we equate the prospects for limiting strategic weapons with those for reaching some kind of overall trade-off between our effort in defensive systems and a substantial Soviet reduction in land missiles. In making such an agreement we would be trading a still largely unknown asset against a known liability (the large Soviet land missile force). The Soviets would be trading a known asset against an unknown liability, but a liability that makes their present economic planning more difficult and one they fear they might not be able to overcome even if they concentrated on overcoming it at the possible cost of domestic economic reform.

The prospect of an agreement, therefore, rests largely on an approximate balance of one side's hopes and the other side's fears. But five years or so from now, this balance is likely to show signs of erosion. It may turn out that we are strikingly successful in our research and development effort, and that the Soviet Union can neither match this effort nor devise effective countermeasures. In that event, we might prove much more unwilling than today to compromise our effort. More likely is the prospect we have already argued for, namely, one in which our efforts are moderately successful but are nevertheless roughly matched or otherwise compensated for on the Soviet side. In that case, Soviet fears will partly recede from where they appear to be today. Soviet leadership will probably have already made the painful decision to commit substantial resources to the defensive effort. Having made the decision and braved the initial consequences, the incentive for making other substantial concessions to the West will have been markedly reduced.

If this reasoning has merit, the impact of a substantial U.S. commitment to defensive systems on Soviet incentives to reduce its offensive forces is greater today than it is likely to be in the years ahead. Unless the U.S. effort is attended by early and striking success, our leverage may be expected to decline by the late 1980s or shortly thereafter. Does it follow that we should therefore push toward concluding an agreement along now familiar lines? Advocates have urged that by doing so we would not only be capitalizing on an asset whose value is undetermined but would not really be compromising, let alone sacrificing, this asset. For we might conclude an agreement that broadly confines our effort to the research phase in return for a substantial Soviet reduction of offensive land missiles. Whereas we would have agreed only to slow down an effort that might always be intensified if the agreement was terminated for some reason, Moscow would have sacrificed a very real asset here and now. If this is indeed the case, however, the question arises: why should the Soviets conclude an agreement in which they give up a large, fixed-capital investment for what is only a moderation of our research effort, an effort that by comparison has cost us to date very little? On the other hand, those who view this effort as promising may find that the "bargain" in getting Moscow to surrender a substantial portion of its land missiles is no bargain at all. As they point out, once such an agreement is concluded, it is likely to be difficult to sustain the kind of effort that makes it worthwhile for the Soviets to remain strictly within the limits of the agreement. From this perspective, such an agreement is likely to impose somewhat greater risks for us than it does for Moscow because we will have to wind down an effort that could be quite difficult to pick up again. By contrast, this argument runs, the Soviets will surrender an asset that could be readily re-placed should circumstance or interest so decree. Opponents of this kind of agreement insist that there is no way by which this presumed asymmetry might be compensated for, let alone re-moved. Even in the absence of our experience with the arms-control agreements of the 1970s, it poses a considerable obstacle to a future agreement.

THE IMPLICATIONS OF SDI FOR U.S. FOREIGN POLICY

The prospects for arms control apart, there remains the broader issue of how a move to defensive systems will affect the overall conduct and objectives of U.S. foreign policy. To the supporters of SDI, the general effect of the program will be to give new strength and vitality to our role and commitments in the world. Having once changed the present structure of deterrence, we will be in a position to act with greater confidence and assurance. The short-term effects of SDI will presumably lead to an increase in stra-tegic stability and a strengthening of extended deterrence. The long-term effects, which are expected to result in something close to the restoration of our historic security, will give us a freedom of ac-tion we have not enjoyed since the 1950s.

To critics, the principal effect of the defense effort will be to encourage the illusion that, in the words of one, "Our national safety can be secured by acting alone."[18] From this perspective, SDI betokens the attempt to return to a past that cannot be restored, to a past when we were secure from physical attack and could pursue a unilateralist foreign policy. SDI thus reflects the refusal to recognize that we must learn to live with our adversary and that we have no safe alternative to a political resolution of our differences. And in the pursuit of political, rather than technological, solutions of the great conflict, our major alliances remain as im-portant as ever.

The debate over the likely effects of SDI on foreign policy reveals more than anything else the basic political outlook and disposition of the parties to it rather than their varying assessments of the possibilities of technology. Whereas supporters of SDI are apt to be political pessimists and technological optimists, critics are apt to be technological pessimists and political optimists, at least relatively. The debate reflects above all varying assessments of the nature of the great conflict between the United States and the Soviet Union and the possible means of our safe deliverance from it. The debate has persisted throughout the postwar period. The differences today over the broad implications of SDI on the nation's foreign policy are simply the latest version of it.

Is it useful to go beyond these well-defined and entrenched positions and speculate about the general policy implications of SDI? Only if one also speculates on the kind of success SDI could ultimately enjoy. Here again, a choice must be made among possible future worlds, the choice that has already been elaborated in preceding pages. Thus, I forgo extended speculation on the implications for foreign policy of a world in which nuclear weapons are rendered impotent because we have acquired an effective defense against ballistic missiles and air-breathing conveyances as well. In this world, we would indeed have largely restored our historic security position, for we would no longer be subject to the threat either of nuclear or even conventional weapons carried by missiles or aircraft. Unable to use the air as a medium of warfare, except tactically, we would move back to an age dominated by land and naval forces. Of even greater importance, we would very likely return to a world dominated by conventional balance-of-power calculations. The prospects of entering such a world, however, are so meager and removed in time as to make any discussion of its policy consequences verge on the fanciful.

More realistic, if only by comparison, is the consideration of the general policy consequences of an effective defense against ballistic missiles, an effective defense possessed by both the United States and the Soviet Union. This, too, is a world far removed from the present one. In the judgment of many scientists it will remain an unobtainable world. But suppose it is obtainable. Would it entail significant effects for U.S. foreign policy? The view that it would rests on the argument earlier noted: that bombers, cruise missiles, and any other air-breathing conveyances that may be employed are much slower than ballistic missiles and therefore less suited for surprise attack. They are also considered safer as deterrent forces, given their relatively greater invulnerability and, for bombers at least, their ability to be recalled.

This world, let it be emphasized, would still remain one governed by mutual deterrence through the threat of retaliation. Thus the essential calculus that many, including the president, have found politically hazardous and morally repellent would remain in force. Would it nevertheless be a much safer deterrent system, since its dependence on bombers, cruise missiles, and the like would make it markedly more stable? This, after all, is the critical claim made on behalf of SDI, a claim that is not insubstantial. But even if it is conceded, the other general effects are not easy to discern.

Thus, it is not easy to assess the consequences of the new strategic dispensation for extended deterrence. The claim has been made that extended deterrence would be strengthened by becoming more credible, but the reasons are not apparent. The one change that clearly would strengthen extended deterrence—at least if cold logic prevailed—would be the restoration of something approaching our former invulnerability. But the new dispensation would not restore this; it would instead alter the character of our vulnerability to nuclear weapons. However important for strategic stability generally such alteration may be, its effects in improving extended deterrence do not appear substantial.

These considerations, moreover, simply assume that the effectiveness of a defense against ballistic missiles will in time come to enjoy such credibility as to go virtually unquestioned. Although ballistic missile systems will remain in place for an indefinite period, they will cease to play a role in the calculations of either side because of the common persuasion that in a severe crisis the defense against them would not be put to the test. And it would not be put to the test, presumably, because of the common perception that the defense on either side is reliable in its effectiveness. The likelihood of this perception arising, however, is not a solid one. Thus, it seems we are destined to repeat the now familiar experience of uncertainty over whether meaningful limits can be placed on the use of nuclear weapons. Yet, we will not and cannot know whether a defense system will work—particularly one that is extraordinarily complex and dependent on several new technologies—short of putting it to a test that may prove fatal. This being the case, even a defense system that is viewed as close to perfect in its effectiveness will, in fact, add yet another uncertainty about nuclear war to those we already have experienced. The great gain in strategic stability that such a system is supposed to confer will rest on this uncertainty, an uncertainty that in a severe crisis will depend for its resolution on an even shorter time span than that characterizing the present system of deterrence.

If these are the likely consequences attending what is deemed to be a near-perfect system of defense against ballistic missiles, then we can conclude that the consequences attending a much more modest system will be less significant. And it is, to repeat, a much more modest system that represents the one prospect over which it is useful to speculate. As such, it seems strained to argue that the defense transition will result in a new global unilateralism, let alone in a new isolationism. It may be that in the years ahead, the conduct of U.S. foreign policy and the character of commitments in the world will undergo substantial change. But in this event, it is unlikely to occur because the results of SDI provided what would otherwise have been a missed opportunity. A much more plausible argument is that the same motivations that at least partially account for SDI may also be expected to give rise to significant change in foreign policy. Major change toward a more unilateralist policy, one intent on contracting present commitments, might occur quite independently of the results of SDI. Indeed, if there is a relationship between the two, it would seem to be of the opposite nature. Rather than result from a successful SDI, a more unilateralist and even isolationist policy might follow more expectedly from the failure of SDI because the existing lapse of faith in deterrence would deepen.

It is not likely, though, that the essential role and commitments of the nation will change significantly in the decade ahead. The view that we are at the beginning of a lengthy defense transition does not alter this conclusion, for the results of this transition will in all likelihood leave U.S. foreign policy substantially where it would be without SDI. The stability of the present structure of deterrence may well be enhanced, a not inconsiderable achievement, although scarcely a revolutionary one. In a world marked by a greater commitment to defensive systems, the basic patterns of conflict will nevertheless remain unaltered. The superpower rivalry may undergo some alteration. If it does, SDI will not figure prominently as a cause. Perhaps the greatest potential effect of a defensive transition will be to reassert the primacy of the United States and the Soviet Union in the international system. The transition is bound to illuminate once again, as it is doing now, the great gap that separates the two from the rest of the world, including the rest of the present nuclear powers.

NOTES

1. Lord Zuckerman, "The Wonders of Star Wars," *The New York Review of Books* (January 30, 1986), 32.

2. Leslie H. Gelb, "Star Wars' Advances: The Plan vs. the Reality," *The New York Times*, December 15, 1985.

3. Robert McNamara, "The Military Role of Nuclear Weapons," *Foreign Affairs* (Fall 1983), 79.

4. Second Vatican Council, *Pastoral Constitution on the Church in the Modern World*, December 7, 1965, National Catholic Welfare Conference, 1966. The Pastoral Letter of the U.S. Bishops on War and Peace, "The Challenge of Peace: God's Promise and Our Response," *Origins* 13, no. 1 (May 19, 1983). The quotations in the text are taken from these documents.

5. See Jonathan Schell, *The Abolition* (New York: Alfred A. Knopf, 1984). Similar views have been expressed by others. See, for example, George F. Kennan, *The Nuclear Delusion* (New York: Pantheon, 1983).

6. Presidential Press Conference, March 25, 1983, *The New York Times*, March 26, 1983.

7. Fred Ikle, "Nuclear Strategy: Can There Be a Happy Ending?" *Foreign Affairs* (Spring 1985), 813.

8. Ibid., 817. It will be apparent that the force of Ikle's argument depends, in part, upon a selection of descriptive terms that gives to his two "ingredients" a connotation that does some violence to the actual state of affairs at present while idealizing, if only by implication, past international orders.

9. Ibid., 822–24.

10. Ibid., 816.

11. Quoted from *The Wall Street Journal*, January 2, 1985, excerpt of a speech by Defense Secretary Caspar Weinberger to the Foreign Press Center, Washington, D.C., December 19, 1984.

12. From a January 12, 1985 speech by President Reagan on defensive technology, "Weekly Compilation of Presidential Documents," March 28, 1985, vol. 19, no. 12.

13. Among the more discerning are: "The Origins of 'Star Wars,' " *The New York Times*, March 4, 1985; Don Oberdorfer, "A New Age of Uncertainty...," *The Washington Post*, January 4, 1985; David Hoffman, "Reagan Seized Idea Shelved in '80 Race," *The Washington Post*, March 3, 1985; Frank Greve, "Out of the Blue: How 'Star Wars' was Proposed," *Philadelphia Inquirer*, November 17, 1985.

14. Ikle, "Nuclear Strategy," 823–24.

15. Keith B. Payne, *Why SDI?* (National Institute for Public Policy, 1985), 4.

16. Ikle, "Nuclear Strategy," 820.

17. "The President's Strategic Defense Initiative," The White House (January 1985).

18. Townsend Hoopes, "'Star Wars'—A Way of Going It Alone," *The New York Times*, January 2, 1986.

2.
THE CHALLENGE OF SDI: PREEMPTIVE DIPLOMACY OR PREVENTIVE WAR?

George Liska

With the emergence of space-based defenses as the chief subject of military-strategic debate, the United States stands at the threshold of a new technology whose political implications will extend well into the next century. If these long-term effects are to govern choice among present options, the debate must transcend purely technical questions and seek to anticipate a hypothetical future. Unavoidably tentative at this stage, an inquiry into the implications of the Strategic Defense Initiative for political policies will achieve little if it does not aim for the "big picture." It must not, therefore, be intimidated by the greater rigor of the exact sciences and specificity of technological data but must scrutinize the laws of politics which, while less reliable and compelling than the laws of physics, nonetheless indicate the range of the probable on the strength of historical evidence.

Correcting for biases that stress operational efficacy and technical feasibility is nowhere more important than in the American culture, including the political subculture. It is a culture that typically favors a strictly defined perspective but now faces a question with far-reaching implications for societies with a radically different orientation and hierarchy of values. Embracing a technology such as the one underlying defenses in space in the alleged interest of humanity at large requires taking into account the human factor in its many facets without, for all that, getting mired in pacifist or any other sentimentality.

STABILITY IN NUCLEAR AND PRENUCLEAR SETTINGS

The effectiveness of mutual deterrence in creating strategic stability can be ascribed to the great uncertainty of the outcome of a nuclear exchange. The uncertainty, and its relation to stability, reflects the fact that there is and can be no reliable identification of the requisites of stability in terms of numbers of weapons and kinds of technology alone. Between major adversaries, one man's or side's stability is another's instability just as, as between the United States and its principal allies, the same deployment can be viewed as coupling or decoupling the two theaters of the Euro-American ecumene. Even in the prenuclear military context, the existence of equilibrium (another word for stability or its foundation) could be established in most instances only by inference from the restrained behavior of the main actors, not by counting muskets in one era and mortars or machine guns in the next. In fact, the impossibility of quantifying "power" was the precondition that allowed the balancing mechanism to work as well as it did. If the outcome of a military conflict could be predetermined by precise measurements, the marked initial advantage in ready capabilities that will prompt a state to challenge the existing order would make resistance decidedly unpromising and, therefore, in many instances less likely.

For strategic stability to be more than contingent—to rest on more than uncertainty revealed in cautious conduct—it must reliably inhibit states from employing military means to do the opposite from exploiting a real or imagined advantage: to wit, counteract a radically worsening political situation. Within a halfway rational universe of action, such total or absolute stability obtains when unleashing a military conflict means signing the death warrant of the attacker himself. A "balance of terror" of this kind has been fading, and with it unconditional stability, as the technology of counterforce has progressed to the detriment of strategies targeting populations as the first or last resort. By once again making war thinkable (because it is escalation-resistant even if not escalation-proof), the increasing efficacy of both nuclear and conventional weaponry has reinforced the shift from total stability to one highly susceptible to pressures from the political arena. The importance of that arena increases also insofar as a major power is most likely to initiate war for objectives more psychological or diplomatic than military. To the extent that they intensify political stress while reducing destruction, partial defenses against ballistic missiles are apt further to weaken stability on the nuclear level. A failproof protection of not only retaliatory capability but also population would go one better and, in effect, restore the traditionally unstable conventional military balance.

Without the threat of assured self-destruction, the issue of war as a practical resort returns to its habitual context as a "continuation of policy by other means," to be analyzed by reference to general principles of statecraft. When the future is at stake, the inquiry must reach beyond actually transpired behavior and consider underlying motives and determinants of action. If certain inferences can be drawn from the observed absence of conflict (for example, existence of equilibrium reflecting widespread satisfaction with the status quo relative to the costs of changing it forcibly), what are the commonly operative incentives to conflict? What will make a major power resort to substantial military action against another great power? Immediately at issue is rationality in statecraft, as distinct from the reasonable person's common sense. Moreover, where narrowly pragmatic or strictly military-strategic criteria would stamp certain conduct as irrational, a particular value system growing out of a specific political heritage might not. In particular to be considered is the hierarchy of values generated by a system (such as the classic European) stressing the absolute primacy of corporate autonomy and by a culture (such as the continental European) that is state- rather than homocentric. A social ethic emphasizing sacrificial heroism, as distinguished from essentially hedonistic needs, will further reinforce the primacy of the state; and this primacy will be portentous in its implications when coupled with a political culture (such as the East European ones, including Russian) whose tendency is to project menacing trends pessimistically into a future jeopardy to be forestalled in the present from still available strength.

Even before the nuclear age set in, great-power regimes had gone to war increasingly for essentially defensive (or preclusive) rather than unqualifiedly offensive (or predatory) reasons. They acted militarily not so much to aggrandize themselves further as to survive as great powers according to the standards of the age.

The last purely acquisitive war, Prussia's mid–eighteenth century conquest of Silesia, was initiated as a means of becoming a great power, whereas Austria's diplomatically aggressive counteraction was designed to recover the lost province in order to restore the empire's standing in the Euro-Germanic theater. Similarly motivated was France's self-assertion on the continent and globally, then and increasingly after 1815 and 1871. All parties to World War I acted for reasons they thought to be, and that largely were, defensive. In a state system that was itself aging, the fear, well-grounded or not, of irreversible decline could not but produce a deep insecurity in an increasing number of regimes, a condition that made an offensive enactment of an essentially defensive posture more or less compelling. For the British, the threat came from Germany; for the Germans, from Russia; whereas for Austria-Hungary and Russia, and increasingly also for France, fear was largely generated from within, from the prospect of instability in the short run or also organic decline in the long.

When pre–World War II conditions and perceptions are given due weight, even the aggressions of Hitler's Germany to a large extent fit the preemptive model, which finds a classic expression in the strategy of Tojo's Japan. Finally, actions calculated to keep open the path to world power by shutting out unacknowledged competitors, decried as unprovoked aggressors, can be considered defensive. In this category belongs U.S. participation in the two world wars. It differs from earlier American wars waged for territorial aggrandizement within an essentially secure milieu under the banner of manifest destiny.

Notably on the part of the non-American polities, the political conditions of individual well-being and the material conditions of individual livelihood related only secondarily to the dominant statist value of corporate autonomy. They were of moment just enough to sustain the sociopolitical order against debilitating stress. Contemporary regimes may be said to remain all the more sensitive to status issues, the less they enjoy assured stability and security of tenure, while the state-centered ideal continues to predominate among the governed so long as the polity has not achieved the condition of material satiety. If true, even an ostensibly "materialistic" ideology, such as the Marxist-Leninist, and a scientific-technological bias, such as that of the Soviet regime and political culture, do not significantly alter matters. Neither feature abolishes the greater-Russian-than-American propensity to respond forcefully to major threats defined by nonutilitarian criteria. Such threats include hostile denial of a still unrealized claim to national self-fulfillment conditioned by the geography and history of "holy Russia." The nuclear context has not altered the crucial equations any more than can or will any foreseeable implementation of strategic defense in space. In fact, the latter may restore them to fuller applicability.

STRATEGIC (AND POLITICAL) STABILITY AND STRATEGIC DEFENSE

Exploring the policy implications of strategic defense requires distinguishing two stages of the scientific-technological progression: the condition of having arrived at a certain plateau and the process of getting there. In both stages, one must consider how far, if at all, one superpower is ahead of the other.

An actual defensive system is likely to extend in the foreseeable future only to the protection of strike forces, constituting terminal or point defense. Such a system, if in place on both sides about equally, could be said to maintain or even increase relative stability contingent on the uncertainty of the immediate consequences of a military engagement. However, such an assessment of deterrence will largely depend on ignoring impulsions from geopolitically focused competitive dynamics and its political-cultural context. When there is a sufficiently strong inducement, a first strike against the offensive or defensive capability of the adversary becomes more attractive than before: while the first strike partially cripples the retaliatory response (makes it "ragged"), even a but limited defense of the initiating side can be expected further to blunt the counterstrike. Stability is preserved only to the extent that the side that has been struck retains "objectively" the capability and "credibly" the will to intensify the exchange, on pain of setting off further rounds of retaliatory escalation. Such a retributory reaction becomes less likely the more one assumes that it would be the party initiating the first strike that was under greater pressure to defend itself offensively and was, therefore, more prepared to incur major damage and run ultimate risks. Under the same hypothesis the side receiving the first strike has less to gain from escalation because it faces the loss of no more than its prior geopolitical advantage. It can look forward to remaining or soon again becoming competitive in both the organic and the diplomatic dimensions of "national power."

More effective defenses aimed at the boost and midcourse phase of enemy missiles are significant in the near future mainly as remotely possible developments. They are all the more threatening to stability if one side is lagging technologically and the technology can be used offensively against command-control-communications facilities. Given the high probability that in an uneven race for improved strategic defense the lagging side would be the Soviet Union, the situation risks enhancing any existing incentives for the Russians to act preemptively before the race was over. Should it by contrast be the Soviets who win a head start in the higher-level defense capability, the incentive to use their advantage before it disappeared would be stronger than any comparable stimulus on the part of a similarly positioned United States. Since Soviet head start is apt to be both precarious and provisional, the likelihood highlights the risks implicit in any arms race when one party expends great effort to match or outstrip a resource-richer adversary only to see the nonrepeatable advantage fade and turn into its opposite unless it is used for a less reversible effect.

Thus, unless one is prepared to hypothesize a situation wherein the balance of both resource-related and geopolitical factors moves clearly from the U.S. to the Soviet side, the Soviets will continue to be the party more strongly motivated to initiate a nuclear exchange. The seemingly optimal state—both sides having a foolproof bubble-like strategic defense over their populations—would only place the United States at a psychopolitical (next to military) disadvantage for a different reason, on the assumption that such a defense would restore the primacy of conventional military force.

Any deterioration in the Soviets' already adverse geopolitical situation would only fuel their urge to act. Since the United States is a saturated conservative power, it cannot be indifferent to the probability that the existence of limited, and the prospect of more advanced, U.S. defenses would make a Soviet first strike more likely. Would the same military-strategic condition enhance U.S. options for offensive (or counteroffensive) self-assertion in the world arena?

In principle, a U.S. effort to exploit strategic defenses politically for a "rollback" would merely increase the pressures on the Soviets to be more aggressive or subversive abroad and to repress or mobilize more intensely at home and regionally. In practice, an offensive U.S. self-assertion on a significant scale would be "rational" only if keyed to major strategic goals worthy of the attendant risks. Among such goals would be the elimination of Soviet dominance in Eastern Europe, using local disaffection from behind the shield of strategic defense. It is most unlikely that the mere possession of a capability would or could be used to push back the Soviets in peacetime. In a more likely contingency, deterrence would have broken down at least partially into a protracted conventional-military conflict. A serious threat to Soviet regional hegemony extending to the Soviet homeland would then tend to elicit a matching assault on the territorial United States, a substantial escalation apt either to overcome less-than-perfect defenses of military installations or to bypass them via countervalue strikes. Comparable, if less drastic, scenarios can be envisaged with respect to other focal areas, such as those abutting on the Persian Gulf.

The hypothetical scenarios point to the real danger latent in partial defenses, even if these are on balance favorable to the United States. They could tempt the leader of the West into theater strategies that promised spectacular results, while being inherently unpredictable as to their military and political effects locally as well as globally on foe and friend alike.

At issue is fundamentally the relation of strategic defenses to offensive political or politico-military behavior at the peripheries of either of the superpowers or the global system itself. It can be (and has been) argued that both of the superpowers seek an advantage in defense sufficient to neutralize the adversary's nuclear capability. The difference begins when the aggressive-expansionist Soviets are said to equate stability with possessing the advantage as a shield not so much against a hypothesized U.S. first strike (as they would claim) but for releasing superior instruments and techniques of lower-level violence for safe employment on behalf of an offensive self-assertion at their and the system's periphery. In the same interpretation the United States as a status quo power needs the advantage for retaining the ability to stage defensive political or nonnuclear military action abroad. Leaving aside the ambiguity of the distinction between offense and defense, the argument points to a glaring asymmetry between routinely limited geopolitical goals to be achieved incrementally and an imminent possession of qualitatively upgraded military-strategic means. The question remains: Would achievable defenses in themselves impart a sufficient advantage to either side to alter substantially the cost-benefit calculations in regard to moderate, at best, gains in mostly inessential areas or on marginal issues? Would they raise sufficiently the nuclear threshold? Or would the peripheral issues continue to be approached and decided on the basis of locally available conventional capabilities and, if in terms of a balance, then one weighing the relative importance of competing national interests and the relative strengths of supporting communal will rather than high-technology military instruments?

GEOHISTORICAL CONSTRAINTS AND EXTENDED DETERRENCE

Hypothetical scenarios will unavoidably proliferate so long as the U.S. (or Soviet) security community is primarily interested in short-term perspectives on tactical or technical military settings of policy and continues to defy the theoretically conceded disutility of nuclear weapons for achieving results offensively. The presumption against usability is unlikely to be significantly altered by presently conceivable technological innovations. Moreover, to repeat, conclusions or inferences drawn from purely military scenarios about the utility of this or that kind of defense will be flawed so long as they rest on assumptions about Soviet geopolitical objectives and behavior that, bemused by the imputation of a world-conquering goal, ignore the more real fundamental issue of survival in great-power role and status.

As terror oozes out of the deterrent balance via counterforce and defense capabilities, the weight of geopolitical (including geographically conditioned historical, or geohistorical) factors necessarily increases. And as the latest American defense initiative injects high drama into the U.S.-Soviet discourse, the time span within which controversial issues and the relationship itself can be constructively addressed grows shorter.

An enhanced capacity to defend retaliatory facilities may well give the United States a diplomatic advantage over Soviet Russia. However, it risks inverting the larger psycho- and geopolitical equations to the United States' detriment. So long as Russia is exposed to confinement between the United States (and Western Europe) and China (and Japan), and especially if the encirclement shows signs of tightening and the comparative development ratios worsen (for example, by virtue of U.S.-aided industrial buildup of China), the incentives will grow for the Soviets to arrest the adverse drift before it is too late. Moreover, just as the Soviets might acquire the stronger incentive to act preemptively by virtue of negative trends, they are likely to retain the greater positive capacity to absorb damage to population and other material assets owing to their communal culture and political system. A political culture that absorbed the loss of twenty million in World War II and was, if anything, morally invigorated by the bloodletting, is on the face of it psychologically fit to face up to a nuclear exchange. It may be better equipped for the ordeal than a society that has been spared any comparable testing throughout its existence, that recently lost its nerve under the stress of casualties in the tens of thousands, and that tends to be traumatized by terror- and accident-induced casualties in the hundreds or less.

By the same token, the temptation for the Soviets to act "while there is still time" becomes an imperative once their options begin to narrow in relation to a neighbor (China), which, more hostile than is the United States and gaining in the capacity to inflict matching damage, exhibits a political and communal culture even more capable of absorbing human and material devastation than Soviet Russia. Tolerance for the loss of life increases along the west-to-east culture spectrum, while impediments to civil-defense preparations decrease. In such a setting anything that might set off a controlled nuclear exchange, only to risk degenerating into an uncontrolled one, constitutes an unevenly weighted deterrent working against the United States in the short run and against Russia in the long. It adds to the hypothetical cost of space-based defenses.

Less hypothetical are the political costs of enhancing U.S. defenses insofar as the attendant dangers would need to be forestalled by appeasing the Soviets politically. To achieve the necessary calming effect in time to avert an impending crisis, the geopolitical setting would have to be reshaped both abruptly and drastically. In the likely absence of compensating Soviet adjustments, the entailed diplomatic revolution would affect adversely U.S. alliances at the center as much as U.S. containment policies at the periphery of the global system. Conversely, absent the ''appeasement,'' instead of staging a technological ''breakout'' via an unmatched SDI equivalent of their own, the Soviets might more plausibly try to break out of the ring of geopolitical encirclement. They could do so in either direction: through China, possibly by way of a surgical or wider strike using Moscow's nuclear advantage while it lasts; or through western Europe, most probably by means of a limited conventional thrust dramatizing the Soviet perception of the developing configuration as lastingly intolerable.

Short of such an extremity, the development of strategic defenses by the United States will still have a profound effect on its alliances and, equally important, on Soviet conduct with respect to those alliances. As the United States develops a more independent capacity to protect its own territory, its stake in extending deterrence to allies will decline even if its ability remains intact or grows—and it will be perceived as declining by ally and enemy alike. So long as Western Europe is less effectively defended than the territorial United States—a situation unlikely ever to change despite parallel defenses against shorter-range Euromissiles—the Soviets will aim pressure or action in the direction of their nearer neighbors. Should such action take a military form, an effectively defended United States would be perceived as being able to defer a climactic confrontation with the Soviets indefinitely while buttressing further its extra-European alliances.

The temptation to sidestep irreversible decisions grows with the ability to defer them. This cliché cannot but impress, and its implications discourage, America's Western allies if U.S. defenses grow faster than those of both the Soviets and themselves. Intra-alliance stress would only intensify if a raised nuclear threshold (due to inter-superpower defenses and/or nuclear force reductions) increased emphasis on conventional-military buildup and related expenditures. Unlike the United States, the politically weak West European governments and their strongly economics-minded publics would rather live dangerously under the shelter of mutual assured destruction (MAD) than slowly atrophy from the strains and costs of adequate conventional or any other defense. Increasing the role of air-breathing delivery systems, such as bomber-carried cruise missiles, in conditions of antiballistic missile defense would not fundamentally alter the intra-alliance equation. The long travel time of such weapons, which makes them susceptible to recall, multiplies occasions for exerting psychological pressure on U.S. allies, who will be responsive to popular anxieties because they have representative governments and who will be free to respond because they are members of a noncoercive multimember alliance. This dual susceptibility augments the Western handicap in relations with an adversary not only comparatively immune to similar pressures but capable of manipulating the scope of military initiatives and the presentation of political intentions in ways calculated to sharpen dissent from radical deterrence or defense on the part of the more vulnerable side.

If extended deterrence is subject to weakening in relation to Western Europe, it is apt to fade in relation to China even before taking on a clear shape. To compensate, a partially and preferentially defended United States might soon see itself compelled to reassure a volatile eastern protégé as much or more than the more solid Western partners. The compensations might be no less military-strategically irrational for being seemingly reasonable (because necessary) politically. The most ironic consequence of upgrading China's military resources and militarily relevant industrial-technological potential might then surface only gradually. Whereas strategic defenses have been initiated against Russia, their development might be eventually vindicated against the furthermost eastern power, positioned as the next challenger in the process.

ARMS CONTROL AND CONTROLLED COMPETITION

It is conceivable that the danger of an uncontrolled competition over strategic defense could lead the superpowers to coordinate its development within the framework of a fresh approach to arms control. However, concerted progress in a militarily critical technology seems impossible without prior or at least concurrent movement toward political accommodation. The military-strategic competition, despite its superficially autonomous dynamics, remains a mere reflection and symptom of relations in the geopolitical base. This does not mean that pressures emanating from a dramatically new phase in the military-strategic sphere cannot extend into the geopolitical theater and create there new incentives and possibilities as well as accentuate existing perils. Any Soviet gains that would result from continuing to extend a previously conceded military-strategic parity incrementally into the geopolitical sphere would be marginal when compared with the adjustments that might be necessary to neutralize the explosive effects of disparate developments in strategic defenses. Moreover, barring a growing disparity of that kind, Soviet self-restraint would be apt to grow as the Soviets developed a stake in the consensually revised order, resting on a henceforth legitimized access to areas and transactions critical for the dispersion of material and military capabilities among lesser regional powers within an evolving international system.

Mutual confidence-building behavior in the sphere that counts most in the final analysis, that of geopolitical competition, would inevitably extend to arms control. The latter's principles and provisions could begin to deemphasize quantitative levels of current weapons allocations and deployments. Instead, they would address primarily the middle- to long-term intentions of the superpowers in regard to research and development initiatives planned in support of their specific security strategies. Such long-term planning is inseparable from the aims pursued in the geopolitical arena. Consequently, a halfway serious attempt to coordinate weapons developments would not only reflect the degree of current consensus but also generate supplemental inducements to concert political policies. It might accelerate the convergence of more fundamental foreign-policy postures to culminate in the sharing of potentially disruptive scientific and technological innovations as they took shape and before they irreparably unbalanced political relationships.

Just as isolating the evolving military instruments from the larger context in the stage of preliminary planning may create new dangers, so conjugating arms development with corrective policy dynamics can open up new opportunities. Optimum defense technologies can mature only in the remote future. But they might still be focused upon now because intermediate improvements would not be sufficient to warrant diverting resources and attention from the eventual optimum. By the same reasoning, political strategies might usefully be keyed to the long-term best in U.S.-Soviet relations, in preference to problematically enhancing questionably vital American interests at the cost of making the relations more antagonistic than they are, or need be, when judged by the standard of uncontestably valid stakes.

However far in the future the positive or negative outcomes might mature, the basic decisions are apt to be taken in the remainder of the present century and some at least in the present decade. The contingency to avoid most—by creating the impression of it being the unchanging U.S. objective—is demotion of the Soviet adversary that compounds the risks from tactical rollback and strategic encirclement. Although the costs to the United States might be greatly deferred, they could still be more than materially devastating. The moral burden is greatest on a polity that has had the less immediate or compelling reason to set the stage for the military resolution of a conflict, should it come to pass for reasons not wholly free of its prior responsibility. In such a perspective, it would be reckless to proceed with the planning and development of defense technologies that (1) do not guarantee a substantial net increase of defense over defense-suppressant or offensive capabilities and (2) are conceived and deployed in isolation from the largest possible psychopolitical context, one made up of divergencies in geopolitical situations and both communal and political cultures.

U.S. preference is for technological and organizational shortcuts to the solution of political problems rooted in ambiguities spanning space and time, geography and history. The impatience has been saved so far from spawning a major catastrophe, let alone a terminal one. In fostering this immunity, the U.S. margin for errors has exceeded the measure of foresight and the quality of design mobilized on America's behalf. It may be that if the latest of Pandora's boxes is opened recklessly too wide, it will disclose a hidden mechanism for evil stronger than the good fortune of history's most favored people. It would then not suffice that it was one of the luckiest political leaders ever who first set the challenge to Fortune in motion.

RESTATEMENTS AND ELABORATIONS

Basic to the U.S.-Soviet relationship is the projection of each party's fears and ambitions onto the other, resulting in the mutual attribution of aggressive intent. In the Marxist view, "internal contradictions" in capitalism make the West "objectively" the aggressor. They will eventually induce—if not force—the leading Western power to strike out first to improve its ability to survive among the competing and less militarily burdened capitalist economies. The propensity of the American ethos to emphasize (material) damage limitation in choosing between alternative strategies would not, in such a doctrinaire view, withstand compulsions from the military-technological advantage vanishing amidst accelerating fiscal or widening economic stress. However, ideological self-exculpation to the contrary notwithstanding, the Soviets, too, face conditions that make them susceptible to a first strike should threats from East or West undermine the chief basis for the regime's claim to internal legitimacy: Russia's position as a world power. If the Western powers increasingly define survival primarily in quantitatively assessed human and material terms, the Soviet embodiment of Russia as a nation built around the state looks first and foremost to the qualitative factor of role and status. Yet again, despite differences in basic mind-sets, either superpower could be impelled toward the abyss of war by a valid kind of strategic rationality, one that meets the test of minimizing loss rather than maximizing gains. The resulting calculations may well prevail under sufficient stress over the contrary counsels of a prudence construed as nothing more profound than risk-avoiding caution.

In terms of historical analogies, a Soviet preemptive strike—and the political culture motivating it—would replicate Japan's offensively defensive response at Pearl Harbor to the prospect of an unmatchable U.S. naval buildup (combined with geopolitical and economic denial). Future U.S. behavior could be tentatively inferred on the same principle from the importance of economic incentives behind America's entry into World War I and II (interest in recovering Allied debts in the first conflict and in frustrating the German bid for succession to Britain's imperial assets and advantages in both). More pertinent is the analogy with the pre–World War I Anglo-German naval competition. Like the British dreadnoughts, defense in space raises military technology to a qualitative, higher new level, restarting the arms race, as it were, from zero and reducing the value of the previous generation of weapons. One perceived result is to elevate the two main competitors categorically over other parties, just as the Anglo-German naval race overshadowed the resources as well as the stakes involved in the receding Anglo-French and Anglo-Russian naval competitions. Another consequence, more galling for the Soviet Union than it was for Germany, lies in reopening the issue of military-strategic parity.

For the Russians, as for the Germans earlier, the purpose of achieving (or closely approximating) such parity was to advance, by one stroke, a twin goal: to deter the established rival for the sake of military self-protection and to exert pressure on it as part of an expansive design aimed also at geopolitical parity. The similarities may be potent enough to outweigh a difference. Rapid technological change endangers the effort to attain and maintain parity most for an eastern power. Such a power tends to favor size and scale over versatility in weapons, more germane to the Western polity: to wit, specifically, Soviet missiles with superior throw-weight capacity, as against the U.S. triad stressing seaborne and air-breathing deterrents. Thus, also, before losing out to Rome, the eastern Mediterranean Hellenistic powers futilely enlarged the Greek military instruments (four- to five-deck ships in lieu of smaller and more mobile three-deck ships, just as war elephants were used in lieu of only human phalanxes), while overly large and immobile Ottoman siege guns proved no match for the western powers' mobile field artillery. Soviet gigantism in weaponry, too, would in the end prove much less effectual within an environment dominated by antimissile strategic defenses.

Meanwhile, the U.S.-Soviet conflict parallels the Anglo-German pattern most alarmingly by stimulating fears and encouraging mutual suspicions of surprise attack. The real surprise might eventually come, for better or worse, from the high-technology nuclear weapons that generate so much concern on both sides playing as small a role in actual combat as the dreadnoughts did in World War I. The impracticality of actually using the "ultimate" weapon would then result in a shift to lower-grade weapons, such as directed conventional munitions, performing the substitute role of torpedo boats and light cruisers.

Should strategic defense play a key role in decreasing the importance of nuclear weapons in favor of conventional forces, U.S.-West European relations might face even greater political strains as more of the burden of matching Soviet conventional strength fell on the European allies. The cohesion of the Atlantic coaltion, like that of any hegemonic alliance, requires that the protection provided by the leading ally exceed the ally's provocation of the enemy. The level of U.S. protection of Western Europe might well decline if strategic defenses shielded mainly U.S. territory while they reduced Washington's incentives to run the ultimate risk for Europe's defense. As for provocation, it might, in unbalanced conditions of defense, emanate not only from the U.S. side directly but from related developments on the German side of Russia's two-front situation that makes Russia (and its clients) vulnerable to territorial revision. Should the Soviets respond with nothing more serious than their own version of strategic defenses, it would substantially undermine the French and British nuclear deterrent forces, further aggravating the no-win situation for NATO's European members. Just as European military security and diplomatic status risked being substantially degraded in a peace that has been made more precarious, so the potential for physical survival would not be enhanced in a war that has become more likely. In these conditions the strategic defense initiative might well point less to a pot of gold at the end of the envisioned rainbow than to the end of the alliance itself.

On the extended East-West spectrum, China has begun to be for Russia in this century, and will be increasingly in the next century, what the Russian empire was in the nineteenth for the Germans and what Persia had been for the Ottoman empire still earlier. When the more centrally located polity confronts the day's principal western power, it typically interacts strategically with the western power or powers as an occasion and impetus for imitating innovative technologies. These are equally or more useful or necessary for dealing with the comparatively backward, but more directly threatening and instinctively feared, power still farther to the east. In the present setting, just as deploying intermediate-range missiles has been more important for the Soviets' undermanned Asian theater than the European theater, so current and future Soviet antiballistic missile defenses are likely to have a similar bias.

How explosive the eastward bias will be, and how intense the preemptively defensive Soviet urge in the western direction, will depend on the prospect for a cooperative transition to a defense-reliant world between the superpowers, attended by political accommodation. Just as any trade-off between U.S. and Soviet assets and liabilities in various regions of the globe is impossible on a one-to-one basis outside an overarching global bargain, so arms-control transactions can be neither individually satisfying nor cumulatively productive so long as they merely trade individual weapons or weapons systems against one another. The "trade" must be the most comprehensive one possible if it is to link present capabilities to compatible concepts of the future.

Near-utopian correctives to competitive power politics become possible only when they are no longer necessary to forestall serious conflict. This truism was progressively revealed as a truth in connection with the League-of-Nations type of a collective security system. It applies equally to apolitical approaches to conflict and security, characteristic of single-minded arms-control efforts. They threaten to elevate a mere procedure that is not even an ongoing process to the status of panacea, while in fact harboring a dangerous illusion insofar as it fails to relate military capabilities consciously to political intentions.

The issue becomes acute whenever efforts at arms control escalate to schemes for substantial reduction, nearing elimination, of strategic nuclear weapons centered on intercontinental ballistic missiles. In contrast to an incrementally evolving politico-military concert attended by weapons coordination, such a leap of faith into the unknown sidesteps the resulting imponderables for strategic stability—unless, of course, the military-strategic and -technological turning point is recognized as entailing repercussions in the geopolitical arena sufficiently far-reaching to actualize its symbolic significance. In the absence of wide-ranging political accommodation, the issue of possible bad faith and deception on one side or the other cannot but inhibit the implementation of a reduction-to-elimination design that equals totally effective strategic defense in transferring prime dependence from nuclear weapons to conventional military weaponry. Related concerns will almost certainly frustrate the benign expectations from curtailing strategic offense, as will the threatening asymmetry with regard to third parties that are likely to resist a self-denial matching the one bilaterally and (in third-party eyes) collusively agreed upon by the dominant superpowers. Even a partial failure to conform on all sides would require extending the degree of superpower accommodation sufficient

to defuse their competition to a virtual comanagement of the worldwide military-strategic chessboard. In brief, a thoroughgoing U.S.-
Soviet "deal" on strategic defense and offense, to be militarily safe
and politically stable, entails a multifaceted global bargain with
selectively condominium-like overtones of truly revolutionary
proportions.

In making a judgment whether the bargain is feasible and
desirable, the first step is to grasp the nature of the U.S.-Soviet
conflict. Just as the United States does not behave as it does because
it is, in Soviet parlance, imperialist, but rather because it is insular,
so the Soviet Union is better understood as continental than as communist. It follows that the United States is not inherently aggressive
but acts expansively when it seeks to preserve the advantages of
its position first across geopolitical space and now in outer space.
The Soviet response aims to approximate and ultimately match the
defensive advantage of the insular counterpart by all possible
means. But whereas the insular power by nature employs the more
discreet political-economic instruments of persuasion, the less-
favored continental power has to rely on more direct and dramatic
politico-military means. Its appearing all the more aggressive and
expansionist as a result accounts in large part for the temptation
to rationalize the need for hypothetically feasible defense by the
fact of unchanging Soviet aggression. The imputation feeds readily
into the Soviet suspicion that the initiative is but the latest medium
for realizing an unalterable plan for undermining the peaceable
Soviet state.

Similarly, in an earlier era, the Soviets branded NATO as an
instrument for Western aggression impelled by resurgent German
revanchism, when, in fact, the more plausible threat lay in NATO's
politically offensive purposes aimed at the structural weaknesses
of the Soviet bloc. By the same token, U.S. proponents of SDI may
rationalize the need for something like it (as, before, for NATO) by
the need to prevent the Soviets from using an actual or asserted
advantage in intercontinental ballistic missiles (as, before, in
armored divisions and massed infantry) to possess themselves
militarily or only politically of Western Europe and, now, also of
much of the Third World. In reality, NATO was in all probability
no more necessary to prevent a Soviet invasion of Western Europe
than space-based defenses are likely to be required for precluding

cumulative Soviet gains either at the Third World margins or the West European center of the international system. What NATO did accomplish—and it was not negligible at the time—was to impede a precipitate all-out Finlandization of a war-shocked Western Europe, and to do this at a bearable cost in terms of intensifying the emergent conflict. SDI's object of forestalling a Soviet grab at geopolitical parity or more is likely to be fraught with greater risks for a lesser reason.

PRODUCTIVE ACCOMMODATION OR PREVENTIVE WAR?

Why, it might be asked, and to what end pursue geopolitical parity? The simplest answer to that question is another query: Why else attain and for what other end seek military-strategic parity, a condition the United States previously conceded to the Soviets? Beyond that, geopolitical parity (combining increased Soviet presence in Europe with no more drastically decreased U.S. preeminence worldwide) is both an alternative and a possible intermediate stage: an alternative to a contentiously prosecuted balance of quantitatively defined power, continuously raising the issue of one party's predominance so marked as to constitute hegemony; and a stage on the road to inter-superpower partnership, one that helps resolve the dialectic of defense and offense in the technological and strategic-military dimension and disposes of the offense-defense ambiguity in politically critical perceptions, while the parties embark on an evolutionary process pointing toward cooperation and convergence.

For evolutionary convergence to speed up and deepen has meant continuing to replace monocentric Stalinist totalitarianism with a political system that embraces functionally plural technocratic features in response to external opportunities and challenges that neither can nor need be managed militarily. The United States for its part would have to evolve toward modes of formulating and implementing foreign policy that impose longer-term and wider-ranging perspectives on the anarchy of individual and group biases. In that they make a society more flagrantly freewheeling in style than free in substance, the biases inevitably distort the manner of implementing the notion of the national interest. By playing upon the indeterminate content of the "national" and maximizing the particularistic connotation of "interest," they deform the thrust of the superficially similar but intrinsically contrasting norm of the "reason" of "state."

As the key by-product if not principal goal of convergence, a mutually acceptable evolution of the international system cannot have as its goal a world order based only on American-type values. A more plausible goal is an environment that is congenial to the continued validity of the more inclusive—and essentially European-ist—diplomatic culture shared by the two superpowers and supportive of their prolonged viability as major actors among emerging ones.

Within an evolving system, the offense-defense dialectic compounds the interplay between primarily land- and sea-based powers, each offensively defensive in its own fashion. Any provisional resolution of the offense-defense dialectic in the military-strategic sphere will take the form of an institutionalized mix of defensive and offensive technologies and strategic applications, conducive to the moderation of militarily achievable goals. The analogous opposition of insular and continental powers will be periodically dissolved into a multiplicity of more symmetric land- *and* sea-oriented—that is, amphibious—powers, a process already initiated in the transition from the sharp Anglo-German to the more qualified U.S.-Soviet dichotomy as respectively insular and continental.

Thus the Greek and the Italian city-state systems, organized around the land-sea power cleavage, yielded in time to the Hellenistic and the early European pan-Mediterranean systems, composed of unevenly amphibious larger powers. Currently, the transition to a new offense-defense mix in military technology and strategy is already entangled with the initial stirrings of the other transition: from U.S.-Soviet maritime-continental asymmetry, one that has carried the European antecedents forward into the era of continent-wide powers, to a more polycentric world of major amphibious powers.

The development entails some demotion of the Big Two to the profit of not only China but also other aspirants to expanded regional roles. For the superpowers to monitor and channel the diffusion of functionally diversified power into a pattern viable for both is, meanwhile, the alternative to the center of gravity in an updated as well as inverted land-sea power spectrum moving away from both. If Japan replacing the United States as the key insular power and China supplanting Russia as the key continental power, is the scenario that comes first and easiest to mind in that connection, it is not the only possible one over time.

Replacing the land-sea power schism with a polycentric configuration of amphibious powers does not bring a guarantee of eternal peace. Nor would cosmic bliss result from transcending the continental-maritime disparity through outer space, a more fundamental modifier of the traditional cleavage than was air power beginning with World War I and transcontinental missiles have been since World War II. Least promise resides in outer space becoming the locus of permanent defensive or offensive military installations, conceived and emplaced competitively. For the two superpowers cooperatively to manage the dispersion of power on earth and jointly develop new resources in outer space has the more positive potential. More realistic, it is also a more inspiring goal than is one of merely denuclearizing an unresolved conflict. Space-based defense, notably when advocated in the millenarian version bound to arouse apocalyptic visions on the Soviet side, injects an unnecessary irritant into an unavoidably precarious and protracted process of evolution. If the politics of such evolution are to contain the side effects of a multistage military-technological revolution, they must be nursed with the patience genuine conservatism owes to all organic change—not least when it involves bodies politic with constitutions that, markedly disparate in outward forms, are equally a historically validated outgrowth of distinctive conditions and situations.

The constituents and the promise of a strategy that promotes processes of change that heal old wounds, rather than opening new ones, must first assume a discernible shape on earth. Only then can any incidental benefits and the consummating reinforcements become manifest in outer space. There is nothing wrong with gradually developing a new defensive-offensive mix in both inner and outer space. On the contrary, such a development can be desirable if it promotes stability by enhancing the uncertainty of military outcomes, not least in regard to a first strike and a whole range of third parties that are harder to deter and penalize than either of the contemporary superpowers because they are hardier in either cultural or material makeups. The wrong sets in when military deterrence is outmatched by psychopolitical "impellence": when one side is swayed toward running a more than hypothetical risk of annihilation in order to preclude a not necessarily greater possibility that the other side is alone about to achieve the capacity for strategic compellence, by virtue of developing complete invulnerability against the key weapon on which deterrence rests. The asymmetry deepens when the challenge offered dramatically in the skies combines with a policy designed to perpetuate also the geopolitical inferiority of an ambitious rival: when, that is, the objective is to make a fiat from the heavens consolidate the rewards of meritorious works performed on earth.

The problem of sin assumes a secular face in world politics when the quest for an abnormal measure of protection by one party spells unbearable provocation for another, inviting desperate reaction. In the guise of a preventive war, such a reaction is inspired less by the expectation of success over the rival party than by the urge to avoid surrender to an irreversible process. The question of expediency rests then, more fundamentally than on the probabilities of the immediate outcome, on the predictability of larger developments over a longer period of time: Can prediction be based on the projection of current trends? Is a present generation either obligated or entitled to run the risks of violent death to ensure bearable living for the next? As political expediency becomes indistinguishable from moral validity, the arrogance of the party that strikes out consists of acting to prevent a future it cannot know. The yet greater conceit is of the side that, failing to ask itself similarly pertinent questions before creating the situation calling for the fatal choice, has presumed to take upon itself the very shape of fate.

3.
THE IMPLICATIONS OF SDI FOR U.S.-EUROPEAN RELATIONS

Robert E. Osgood

The Strategic Defense Initiative is not the first U.S.-backed military program to have caused significant concern among the European allies and major controversy between the U.S. and allied governments or their publics. So did the deployment of Thor and Jupiter missiles in Europe between 1959 and 1964; the proposal to create a multinational nuclear force (MLF) between 1960 and 1965; the 1960s campaign that led NATO to adopt a policy of flexible and controlled response in 1967; and the plan to deploy intermediate-range nuclear forces (INF) in Europe, beginning in 1979. Each of these touched a sensitive nerve in U.S.-allied relations, but none touched so many as SDI.

The MLF and INF controversies were more sharply focused and—in terms of European interallied tensions (in the case of MLF) and domestic conflicts (in the case of INF)—more intense than SDI has yet become, if only because SDI is still in the research stage. The U.S. effort to strengthen NATO's conventional capabilities to support a strategy of flexible response to Soviet aggression activated some of the sensitive strategic issues that SDI has raised anew. But only SDI has impinged the whole range of issues that have bedeviled allied security and cohesion: issues of military strategy (including the conventional-nuclear relationship and U.S. extended nuclear deterrence), arms control, East-West relations, defense expenditures, technology sharing, and the independent British and French nuclear forces.

TOWARD CRISIS OR ASSIMILATION?

The controversies touched off by SDI are deep-rooted. They will be with us for a long time. But they can be absorbed without precipitating another crisis within NATO. They may grow more intense if they become focused on the procurement and deployment of specific weapons for the United States or NATO or if they become central to arms-control policies on which differing U.S. and allied priorities and differing views within Europe are a matter of lively domestic political contention. But over the next five years or so only the prospect of sharing the research and development of SDI technology is likely to affect relations within NATO. The allies may find their share of SDI technology disappointing, but SDI is not the stuff of crisis and could even become a source of cooperation.

Eventually, SDI, as a leak-proof population-defense system, may well run its course and fade away, like the MLF, for a combination of technological, economic, and political reasons. But as a system to defend a variety of land-based military targets in Western Europe as well as the United States, and perhaps as a system offering partial defense of national populations, SDI, like the flexible-response doctrine and INF, will probably be assimilated during the next two or three decades into the East-West arms competition and the familiar pattern of intra-alliance relations. This means that the alliance will adjust to U.S. SDI deployments and will absorb SDI and related technologies (notably, antitactical ballistic missile [ATBM] technology) through the normal process of give-and-take by which the allies have absorbed other military programs with major strategic implications. Given the compelling framework of mutual interests at the core of the alliance, assimilation is likely with or without a comprehensive arms agreement limiting strategic defense weapons and reducing strategic nuclear warheads. But without such an agreement the transition to a more balanced offense-defense mix is bound to upset East-West relations and, possibly even more, West-West relations.

An assimilated SDI would constitute a landmark in the evolution of NATO's military posture, but it would not transform the alliance. It would not overcome the dilemma of Europe's dependence on nuclear deterrence, which compels the allies to embrace and reaffirm the U.S. nuclear protectorate even though, given the specter of nuclear war in Europe, they are as fearful as they are doubtful that it would be used in their behalf. Within the existing structure of qualified U.S. military hegemony, this dilemma can be only occasionally alleviated but never resolved, and the existing structure has proved very durable. Realistically, therefore, the policy implications of SDI for U.S.-allied relations fall within the range of things that may aggravate or alleviate NATO's nuclear dilemma, although SDI's ultimate goal is to solve the dilemma by abolishing nuclear deterrence. Nevertheless, SDI, assimilated or not, could aggravate rather than mitigate this dilemma. Indeed, its initial impact sent a sharp shockwave throughout NATO. The potentially disruptive effect of SDI on U.S.-European relations is now muted only because the program is still in its formative stage, far short of deployment, and because its full implications for arms control, whether as an obstacle or a lever, are only beginning to unfold.

THE CONTEXT OF EXTENDED DETERRENCE

The principal measure of the significance of SDI for the West Europeans and their relations with the United States is the same measure as in other interallied controversies and crises: the extent to which it affects, and the way it affects, the role of extended deterrence—that is, the extension of U.S. nuclear deterrence to the protection of its allies from Soviet aggression and intimidation—in NATO relationships. The credibility and acceptability of this deterrent are at the core of NATO's security and cohesion.

Extended deterrence poses a dilemma, not just a problem. On the one hand, the allies are unwilling—if not, strictly speaking, physically and economically unable—to develop the kind of conventional resistance capabilities that could stop an all-out conventional attack by the Warsaw Pact at the eastern frontier of West Germany; so they depend on the U.S. will to initiate the use of nuclear weapons as a compensatory deterrent. On the other hand, as the Soviet capacity to retaliate with nuclear blows against the United States has increased, the credibility of the U.S. commitment to start a nuclear war to protect Europe has come into question; but the unacceptability of a nuclear war, or for that matter a conventional war, in Europe has never been in question. So the European allies chronically suffer from twin fears of U.S. desertion: the fear that the United States might not be willing to use nuclear weapons to protect them and the fear that the United States might be willing to use nuclear weapons in Europe but not against the Soviet homeland. The United States, conversely, has the chronic task of reassuring its allies that the United States will honor NATO's nuclear first-use commitment while urging the allies to strengthen their conventional forces so as to minimize the necessity of carrying out the commitment.

The strategic dilemma, although insoluble within the prevailing transatlantic structure of the alliance, is, except in passing crises, quite tolerable because the actual danger of a Warsaw Pact attack seems infinitesimal, particularly in comparison to the threat during the Berlin blockade, at the outbreak of the Korean War, or during the second Berlin crisis of 1958–61. Consequently, in practice, the convenience of relying on a nuclear first-use strategy overshadows the anxieties and tensions that this expedient incites. Living with the dilemma is made easier for the allies because they profess to see little difference from the standpoint of their national survival between a nuclear and a conventional war. Living with the dilemma is made easier for the United States because it is a moderate price to pay for maintaining allied solidarity—especially to sustain West German cooperation and constraint—and because solidarity is itself a potent deterrent and diplomatic counter to the Soviet Union.

Nevertheless, the dilemma, to one degree or another—depending on Soviet actions, changes in the East-West military balance, and other political and military circumstances—is a constant source of tension. The United States and its allies have tried to mitigate this tension through a series of transatlantic bargains and adjustments. Considering the compelling common interests the allies have in maintaining allied cohesion—principally, military security, diplomatic strength, and the ability to manage the "German problem"—there is every reason to think that this fairly harmonious process of mitigation will continue. But several developments in the past fifteen or twenty years have accentuated the dilemma and raised questions about long-term Western security. These developments amplify the potentially disturbing impact of SDI:

1. The expansion of Soviet strategic and theater nuclear capabilities since the mid-1960s has been accompanied by the substantial

strengthening of the Warsaw Pact's conventional blitzkrieg capacity. This is in accordance with Soviet emphasis since the late 1960s on preparation for an initial conventional war in the European theater, in conjunction with the deployment of mobile and less vulnerable theater nuclear weapons intended to neutralize NATO's nuclear first-use option. Soviet enhancement of conventional capabilities increases NATO's dependence on the early use of nuclear weapons, whereas Soviet enhancement of tactical nuclear capabilities further deters NATO's resort to nuclear weapons in a conventional war. And these developments take place when budgetary stringencies impede meeting existing force-goal commitments, let alone strengthening conventional forces.

2. The INF deployment crisis revealed and accentuated the impact of popular nuclear anxieties in Western Europe, mobilized by political activists—with particular effect in the German Social Democratic and British Labor parties—against nuclear programs and in favor of arms control and détente. Associated with this phenomenon is a threefold attack on nuclear deterrence: the moral attack led by the churches, the ecological attack led by scientific publicists of Nuclear Winter, and the strategic attack led by technical skeptics of the feasibility of limiting and controlling nuclear exchanges.

3. In 1980 the U.S.-Soviet détente collapsed following the Soviets' occupation of Afghanistan; meanwhile, the allies, especially the West Germans, tried to maintain the East-West détente in Europe. These events accentuated the difference between U.S. and European approaches to the Soviet Union in this period and placed the onus on the United States to revitalize the policy of containing Soviet expansionism. In order to allay European anxieties, to secure support for military programs to strengthen NATO, and to counter Soviet efforts to exploit U.S.-allied differences, the United States turned to intensified efforts to negotiate arms control. But whereas the absence of active East-West arms-control negotiations raises European anxieties and heightens everyone's longing for détente, the activation of arms negotiations, especially when they involve the European theater, is likely to accentuate differences of strategic perspective between the United States and the European allies—notably, the differences arising from Europe's dependence on the U.S. nuclear deterrent and from its greater vulnerability to Soviet attack.

These developments reveal the anxious ambivalence with which the European allies view the slightest sign of a weakening of will on the part of the United States to couple its full nuclear deterrent to their defense. The allies also threaten to confront any major new military program, especially one that would alter the nuclear balance, with organized popular opposition. To counter these effects the United States presses its allies to raise NATO's nuclear threshold by strengthening conventional capabilities, and it champions arms control as the centerpiece in the improvement of East-West relations. The administration's cautious peace initiative in Reagan's second term has somewhat softened transatlantic differences over the conduct of East-West relations. But keeping these existing and latent differences under control depends, eventually, on a mutually satisfactory outcome of arms negotiations. Yet the structural and technical obstacles to the achievement of a comprehensive arms agreement have never been greater.

EUROPEAN RESPONSES TO SDI

The intensification of NATO's nuclear dilemma, aggravated by the developments in U.S.-allied relations just outlined, made it certain that any major change in NATO's military posture and strategy initiated by the United States would activate all the strategic anxieties, diplomatic concerns, and transatlantic tensions that the dilemma chronically generates. The substance, method, and timing of President Reagan's enunciation of SDI in March 1983 guaranteed that this program would be extremely disturbing to allied governments.

Proclaimed without previous consultation with (as opposed to notification of) the allies, defined as a program intended to abolish nuclear deterrence, and justified on the highest grounds of morality and international security, SDI burst into public attention as an extraordinarily large research program designed to transform the military foundation of Western security. The presented instrument of transformation was antinuclear shields for both East and West, which would render nuclear weapons "impotent and obsolete" and enable mutual deterrence to depend on the protection of national populations from nuclear strikes instead of on the vulnerability of national populations to nuclear retaliatory destruction. And this proposed strategic transformation, with its implied denigration of nuclear deterrence, was presented to Europe in the midst of the NATO-wide effort, in the face of intense domestic opposition, to deploy intermediate-range missiles on European soil in order to assure the coupling of U.S. strategic nuclear forces to the defense of Europe.

The initial shock with which allied governments reacted to President Reagan's announcement, however, was followed by more complex reactions as the SDI program was shaped by the diverse forces of technological developments, defense budgets, the arms-control dialogue, domestic politics, and prospects of industrial-technological spinoffs. Several conditions have suppressed the initial shock caused by Reagan's announcement, muted official opposition to SDI in Western Europe, and prevented SDI from becoming a focus of popular protest: (1) the abstract and remote quality of SDI's ultimate goal, (2) the prospect that this goal will become practically irrelevant as technological and economic difficulties mount and Reagan leaves the presidency, (3) the fact that SDI is still only a research program, (4) the tendency of different groups and individuals engaged in this program to emphasize a variety of objectives short of creating population shields, (5) the fact that the United States swears adherence to the ABM treaty while it seeks agreed reductions of nuclear strike weapons, including the medium-range missiles in Europe, and (6) official U.S. assurances (as in the Reagan-Thatcher accords) that SDI aims to stabilize a strategic balance, not to achieve strategic superiority, and that the United States will not deploy defensive weapons beyond the ABM treaty restrictions without consulting its allies and negotiating with the Soviets. Moreover, unlike INF, SDI remains largely the concern of governments and experts because it is, for the time being, a set of esoteric technical issues and complicated, hypothetical, strategic, political, and economic issues, which offers a variety of outputs to support but nothing visible to demonstrate against.

Nevertheless, just as the initial European shock in response to the announcement of SDI did not forecast the second wave of reactions, so the second wave seems destined to give way to a somewhat different set of reactions as technological and budgetary factors affect the interplay of defense policies and arms negotiations. Several weapons and arms-control developments could act as catalysts for the recrudescence of initial concerns. But the impact of these developments on U.S.-allied relations will depend very much on how the United States manages the details of its policy responses to them. Whatever these policy responses, however, future European reactions to SDI and their implications for U.S.-allied relations seem likely to fall into the same categories as previous responses. It is important to keep these responses in mind because future developments might again bring them to the forefront of European concerns. Understanding these categories of response to SDI requires distinguishing among them, explaining them, and evaluating them.

Military Security

Universally, allied governments, as soon as they understood that Reagan meant what he said, viewed SDI with dismay on the grounds that, as announced, it would undermine the rationale of extended nuclear deterrence, which had given them forty years of unprecedented peace and security. The French were particularly vehement on this point, just as they have been particularly disturbed by the U.S. emphasis on reducing NATO's reliance on nuclear first-use by strengthening conventional options. Privately they complained that denigrating nuclear deterrence jeopardized the French domestic strategic consensus in support of France's new hard-line military and diplomatic positions under President François Mitterrand.

The corollary of this fear of nuclear nakedness was the fear that rendering nuclear weapons impotent and obsolete would make Europe safe for conventional war. Forced to rely entirely on conventional denial capabilities (and on chemical weapons, in the absence of an effective ban against them) instead of on a conventional "tripwire" or "pause" plus nuclear escalation, the European allies feared that they would either have to spend unaffordable (or, at least, entirely unacceptable) funds on conventional defense, which would still be incapable of withstanding a Soviet blitzkrieg, or be prepared to surrender for the sake of national survival.

Next in prominence among early adverse strategic reactions in Western Europe to President Reagan's SDI proclamation was the fear that shielding Americans from Soviet nuclear attacks would lead the United States to return to Fortress America or, at least, to decouple its strategic nuclear forces from the defense of Europe.

This fear runs directly contrary to U.S. strategic logic and under-estimates the strength of the U.S. self-interested commitment to the security of Western Europe, which crystallized during World War II and has been consolidated by a powerful set of en-tanglements since the creation of NATO in 1949. But the fear is not so implausible as it sounds. Europeans are conscious of the historical correlation of U.S. physical invulnerability with isolationism. More-over, although the growing vulnerability of the United States to Soviet nuclear retaliation may have depreciated the credibility of extended deterrence, the restoration of prewar national in-vulnerability would not necessarily have the opposite effect. There is a great psychological difference between degrees of vulnerability and no vulnerability. Any degree of U.S. vulnerability to Soviet retaliation may give the United States a stake in deterring aggres-sion against Europe, whereas the expectation of invulnerability may relieve the United States of that incentive, especially because the United States has acquired extensive global commitments that com-pete for the support of scarce resources. At least, that is the way anxious Europeans judge the strategic logic of the U.S. commit-ment to their security.

If the American logic that correlates reduced U.S. vulnerabili-ty with the enhanced credibility of nuclear first-use is correct, however, it tends to support a more plausible European strategic anxiety: that the superpowers, protected by national shields, would spare each other from attack while waging a nuclear or conven-tional war in the relatively vulnerable European theater; or at least that Europe's geographical proximity to a great number and variety of Soviet strike weapons would lead the Soviets to concentrate on theater attacks rather than on the less profitable targets in the United States. Although Americans have a material interest in limiting an East-West war to Europe, Europeans are inclined to view any war in Europe as a catastrophic repetition of World War II.

Thus, SDI reawakened all of Europe's chronic strategic anxieties. The intensity of this reaction resulted from President Reagan's em-phasis on the vision of replacing nuclear retaliation with antinuclear protection as the basis of peace and security. If the SDI research pro-gram had been announced as an effort to catch up with the Soviet strategic defense program and guard against a Soviet breakout from the ABM treaty, or even as an effort to explore the feasibility of reducing the vulnerability of U.S. land-based retaliation forces—rationales that were prominent in the U.S. military establishment and national-security community—the adverse reaction would have been less intense and sweeping and SDI might even have attracted some early support among allied governments. Fears would then have focused on the possibility that SDI, given its huge funding and scope, would accelerate the arms race, disturb East-West relations, obstruct an arms agreement, and jeopardize the ABM treaty. But there would have been—indeed, there is now—considerable understanding and support for a U.S. program to reduce the vulnerability of U.S. land-based retaliatory forces, especially if the program was confined to terminal ballistic missile defense (BMD).

A terminal-defense BMD program would be seen as an effort to enhance extended deterrence, rather than as a threat to undermine it (although, by the same logic, some would argue that such a program would also enhance the prospect of a nuclear war confined to Europe). Moreover, if application of SDI and related technology could be extended to the European theater, as the United States has promised, for the purpose of defending military facilities and sites, including INF, this would encourage defense-minded official, military, and corporate leaders in Western Europe to regard SDI as a positive contribution to their own security. For this purpose SDI has been endorsed by Prime Minister Margaret Thatcher, West German Chancellor Helmut Kohl, and Prime Minister Jacques Chirac, the neo-Gaullist who hopes to replace Mitterrand in the 1988 elections. The few prominent private citizens in Europe who praise SDI and advocate it for Europe, such as Lord Chalfont in Britain and General Gallois in France, speak of SDI as land-based terminal defense of nuclear weapons and facilities.

President Reagan's insistence on justifying SDI exclusively in terms of its ultimate goal keeps the initial strategic anxieties alive. Nonetheless, these anxieties have been muted by skeptical second thoughts about the technological and budgetary feasibility of population shields (at least for the next twenty or thirty years); U.S. assurances about maintaining nuclear deterrence as long as necessary; a U.S. promise to consult the allies and negotiate with the Soviets before deciding to deploy new BMDs; European hopes that at least the development and testing of space-based weapons may be banned or suspended in return for nuclear offensive reductions;

favorable (if puzzling) signals from the U.S. bureaucracy and the contracting research laboratories about SDI's more proximate and less worrisome goal of protecting intercontinental ballistic missiles (ICBMs) and command, control, communication, and intelligence facilities (C³I); and, as mentioned earlier, the possibility that when Reagan leaves the presidency the official commitment to his ultimate SDI goal will disappear.

These European second thoughts about the strategic significance of SDI are well advised on practical grounds. They argue for a calm and pragmatic approach to real policy choices instead of the initial alarm in reaction to remote and hypothetical possibilities. But a rounded evaluation should nevertheless consider the implications of these hypothetical possibilities because they will persist as part of the background of allied responses to SDI as long as the U.S. government justifies SDI in terms of the ultimate goal President Reagan proclaimed.

Feasibility of SDI

It is an open question as to whether Europeans could be convinced of the virtue of Reagan's vision of protective shields for Europe and the superpowers if they thought it was feasible and not too costly. Polls in Europe, as in the United States, indicate popular approval of the idea in the abstract. But the fact of the matter is that people in Western Europe with informed opinions about the technological feasibility and affordability of nearly perfect antinuclear shields are almost universally skeptical for all the reasons that induce skepticism among American scientists and technologists. There is equal skepticism about the possibility that the Soviets would help to alleviate the technological problems by cooperating with the United States in fostering a transition toward the ultimate goal through a series of arms agreements that would constrain offensive and antidefensive measures.

Suffice it here to say that profound skepticism about the feasibility of ever achieving nearly perfect shields against all kinds of nuclear attacks seems justified on technological and political grounds. Even if such protection was feasible for the superpowers, extending the same degree of protection to Western Europe would seem technically impossible, considering the variety of Soviet weapons with nuclear (and interchangeable conventional) warheads of all ranges and considering their speed of delivery and mobility. Only if conventional weapons eventually replaced nuclear weapons for all counterforce functions might the problem of Europe's differential vulnerability to nuclear weapons be overcome, but then only at the price of establishing an adequate conventional balance.

The supposition that defensive weapons, in unrestricted competition with offensive and counterdefensive weapons, could be effective enough to render the latter impotent is so highly improbable as to be a foolish basis for the investment of billions of dollars far into the future. Under the most favorable conditions that can be reasonably imagined, nearly perfect shields could be achieved only through the constraints of an extremely comprehensive arms agreement, reached through a series of transitional agreements, that reliably abolished all kinds of nuclear weapons. But everything we know about the difficulties the United States and the Soviet Union had in SALT I and II agreeing on comprehensive limitations of their strategic forces—limitations that essentially only ratified the status quo—militates against the likelihood that these armed adversaries would agree to the radical restructuring of their forces that the ultimate goal of SDI requires.

Perhaps, a better case can be made for 70 or 50 percent effective defensive systems in an offense-defense mix that would leave a minimum number of long- and medium-range nuclear weapons for escalatory and countervalue retaliatory purposes, while counterforce functions were largely performed by conventional weapons. A partial defense against nuclear and conventional missiles would be more feasible; it should be more acceptable to the European allies, especially if they could gain comparable protection to that which the superpowers enjoyed. In the long run a preponderantly nonnuclear and antioffensive military structure may be congruent with the current trend toward the conventionalization of tactical and strategic nuclear forces. But these are hypothetical speculations that cannot be appraised in operational terms for decades.

One thing among these imponderables is particularly clear to Europeans: the prospect of abolishing NATO's familiar nuclear dilemma by constructing a defense-dominant structure of mutual deterrence is not sufficiently promising to justify any diversion from the prior task of making extended nuclear deterrence as credible and reassuring as possible. Toward this end stronger conventional ground and air forces are indispensable, but SDI and SDI-related technology may also have an important role to play in protecting "hard points."

Be this as it may, European skepticism about the feasibility of SDI as nearly perfect defensive shields is warranted. However, the effect of this skepticism on U.S.-allied relations cuts different ways. On the one hand, zealous U.S. championing of such an improbable vision is unsettling to Europeans, who cannot regard a projected $26 billion program (from 1985 through 1989) as just another flight of American utopianism, even if Congress cuts the funding in half. Whether or not the concept of mutual assured defense is infeasible, it will leave its unpredictable imprint on military doctrine, defense budgets, and arms control; and the European allies are upset by change. On the other hand, the incredibility of nearly perfect antinuclear shields encourages allied governments to focus on proximate and real aspects of SDI and hope that the fantasy will fade. In other words, the unreality of the vision helps the allies to accept SDI with equanimity as long as the United States does not push it beyond the research stage.

Again, however, it is important to relate the question of SDI's feasibility to its objective. If the objective was to enhance U.S. land-based nuclear retaliatory forces or to strengthen conventional defense and the nuclear first-use option in Western Europe rather than to shield national populations, the technological problem would be considerably different and SDI much more promising. Indeed, integrated with ATBMs and the "emerging technology" of conventional, precision-guided munitions and C^{3}I for deep interdiction, ABMs and space-based systems might find their most useful application in the European theater. This possibility is considered later in this chapter.

Stability of the Military Balance

Regardless of the technological feasibility or infeasibility of SDI, government and other leaders in Western Europe generally oppose SDI for another reason: its supposed stimulus to the arms race and its allegedly destabilizing effect on the East-West military balance and East-West relations in general. This opposition is particularly intense among left-wing groups. Its most significant impact is in West Germany, where the longing for East-West détente runs strong and the government must make allowances for the latent antimilitary sentiment revealed during the INF crisis—especially because Foreign Minister Genscher is impelled by conviction and the politics of his position in the Free Democratic Party to defer to antimilitary and prodétente sentiment.

In Europe more than in the United States governments tend to defer to popular sentiment in their view of the "arms race" (more accurately, the competition for military strength through quantitative and qualitative improvements in weapons) as an ever-increasing, self-perpetuating, technologically determined accumulation of ever-more-deadly nuclear arsenals, which, if not halted, will lead to Armageddon. Europeans believe that through arms agreements and détente the arms race can be curbed and its dangers suppressed. They regard the Strategic Arms Limitations Talks (SALT) agreements of the 1970s as the most significant remission of the arms race malady, and they are naturally anxious to preserve them. This means, among other things, preserving the ABM treaty's severe restrictions on strategic defense weapons, in accordance with the theory that invulnerable nuclear forces clearly capable of inflicting unacceptable retaliatory damage on vulnerable populations are the best guarantee of peace.

According to this view (which is commonplace in the United States, too, but not shared by the Reagan administration) any proposal to introduce new or additional BMD weapons into the strategic equation, especially if not in the context of a negotiable comprehensive arms agreement, threatens to touch off a new round of the arms race in a mounting defensive-offensive competition and to destabilize the nuclear balance. Space-based BMDs are regarded as particularly pernicious because of the mystique (and myth) of space as a weaponless sanctuary, the extraordinary variety of exotic weapons that space promises to spawn, the uncertain and untestable wartime effects of these weapons and their components operating in conjunction with each other, and the presumed insurmountable vulnerability of such weapons to countermeasures. Furthermore, increasing the proportion of strategic defensive to strategic offensive weapons, it is feared, might mislead one side or the other to think that it possessed a rational first-strike capability because BMD could impair a ragged retaliatory strike. Clearly, the persistent Soviet criticism of SDI on these grounds, coupled with the Soviet threat to counter defensive weapons with an increase in offensive as well as defensive capabilities, reinforces these concerns.

These European concerns, at the least, exaggerate reality. The dynamics of East-West arms competition are much more complex and less ominous than the stereotyped view of the arms race. Budgetary constraints, the general quality of East-West relations, and many other factors, in addition to the invention and production of new weapons, affect the intensity of the arms competition. Despite occasional waves of fear in the United States that new weapons will upset the strategic balance—the erroneous post-*Sputnik* fear of a "missile gap" is the most notable—the history of the post–World War II arms competition shows that technological gains by either side are offset by compensating measures on the other side long before either obtains a decisive advantage. Indeed, the high rate of technological innovation, along with the quantitative surplus of nuclear striking power, makes truly destabilizing weapons innovations—that is, those that dangerously enhance the likelihood of a first strike—quite unlikely, although they may intensify the competition and make it more expensive.

Why, then, should the incremental introduction of BMD into the superpowers' arsenals over the next three or four decades, whether within the constraints of the proposed transitional arms agreements or not, be more destabilizing than the introduction of ICBMs or cruise missiles? To be sure, the element of uncertainty about the actual performance of BMD in warfare would be greater, but logic and common sense suggest that this uncertainty will be a stronger deterrent to the side contemplating a disarming first strike against protected retaliatory forces than to the side retaliating against either counterforce or countervalue targets. If space-based BMDs are substantially more vulnerable to countermeasures than, say, land-based ICBMs, which is not necessarily the case, would their vulnerability attract a first strike against them in a crisis, on the assumption that nuclear retaliation would be less likely or costly? Such a lapse of risk-taking constraint, given the uncertainties of technological performance and adversary behavior involved, seems implausible. If what is envisaged, nevertheless, is a war of attrition in space, such a war would at least seem to be more subject to limitation and early termination than nuclear exchanges on land under current conditions (in which, incidentally, space-based sensors would also be targets).

In so far as reasoned speculation can penetrate the incalculable hypothetical realities of the effect of new and additional BMDs on the arms competition and the military balance, the fears of Europeans and others about the consequences of abandoning the present offense-heavy structure of deterrence seem, at the least, exaggerated. But the fears are nonetheless real and will probably persist, considering the popular anxieties that would be excited by major alteration of the familiar basis of deterrence, which lies in the mutual vulnerability of the superpowers and their allies to retaliatory destruction. European governments and populations regard this mutual vulnerability as both unavoidable and exceedingly dangerous to try to alter.

Only under two conditions might the European allies find it acceptable to increase substantially the proportion of strategic defensive weapons compared with strategic offensive weapons: (1) The change must take place in the context of a comprehensive agreement that promises to curb the arms race and enhance the stability of the military balance. (2) The change must not weaken the credibility of NATO's nuclear first-use strategy or substantially increase the burden of the nonnuclear defense of Western Europe.

Arms Control

As organized popular anxieties about nuclear weapons and weapons competition have increased, strategic arms control—if only in the form of negotiations that hold some promise of an agreement—has become more necessary to allay anxieties and to gain acceptance of major nuclear weapons programs and support of defense budgets. This political truth was both revealed and enhanced by allied insistence on the "two-track" approach to the deployment of INF. It is even more compelling with respect to SDI, which envisages a radical restructuring of deterrence and an extension of the arms competition into a much larger realm of new, more powerful weapons.

Conscious of this role of arms control, the Reagan administration, despite its criticism of the SALT agreements and its skepticism about the utility of strategic arms control, has proposed that the new world of mutual assured defense and survival be achieved in cooperation with the Soviet Union by means of transitional arms agreements. The agreements would begin with the deep reduction of strategic nuclear warheads (and of medium-range nuclear weapons in the European theater), especially on those ICBMs with multiple independently targeted reentry vehicles (MIRVs) capable, hypothetically, of knocking out most U.S. land-based ICBMs on a first strike. The Reagan administration postulates these agreements as steps toward the world of nearly perfect antinuclear shields. Yet all European governments and almost all security specialists devoutly hope that the United States, having helped induce the Soviets to return to the strategic arms talks in order to curb SDI, will use SDI as a bargaining chip by offering to ban development and testing, as well as deployment, of new strategic defense weapons (especially those based in space), and antisatellite weapons (ASATs) too, while reaffirming and tightening up the ABM treaty restrictions.

In addition, some Europeans—especially those in the left-wing parties of West Germany, Britain, and the Netherlands—look toward the elimination or at least an equitable reduction of intermediate-range missiles in the European theater, which the Soviets, before the Reykjavik talks in the fall of 1986, encouraged them to anticipate by separating such cuts from the fate of SDI and dropping their insistence on including British and French nuclear forces among Western medium-range missiles. But other groups in Europe find that things have changed since the INF crisis. Governments are now more worried that a superpower arms deal might "denuclearize" Europe than that it might make Europe more vulnerable to a nuclear attack, and even the antinuclear Left no longer worries so vociferously that INF will endanger the peace.

The Soviets, appreciating the European apprehensions about SDI and European reliance on arms control as an instrument of détente, concentrate on condemning SDI as the sole obstacle to nuclear reductions. So far, they have advocated such reductions on terms that would not actually diminish the first-strike capability of their SS–18 missiles unless their utopia of abolishing all nuclear weapons was achieved. By impressing anxious Europeans (and Americans) with the "generosity" of their concessions on offensive reductions, the visceral appeal of a complete ban on testing of nuclear weapons, and the alluring goal of abolishing all nuclear weapons, the Soviets hope to emphasize all the better the obstacle that SDI poses to arms reductions and détente. Thereby, they hope to stimulate allied and congressional pressure against the program, while exploiting U.S.-allied differences, without having to pay anything in terms of constraints on their own military programs in an arms agreement.

To counter this Soviet tactic the United States must, at least, propose an attractive and plausible (that is, seemingly negotiable) arms agreement and place the onus on the Soviets for rejecting it. At most, it can hope to achieve a satisfactory nuclear arms reduction through another treaty. But such an arms agreement is unlikely so long as the United States lacks carrots or sticks to induce the Soviets to limit offensive weapons (especially, their MIRVed ICBMs), in which they have a quantitative advantage, while the United States holds open the option of eventually deploying defensive weapons, in which it has a technological lead. The United States has no persuasive concession to offer—probably not even a limit on ASATs, which it rejects anyway—so long as it bars any restriction on SDI development and testing that is not consistent with its interpretation of the ABM treaty. Yet as long as the United States is also reluctant to threaten unilateral development, testing, or deployment of SDI beyond the restrictive definition of the ABM treaty, it lacks bargaining penalties to impose. Moreover, even aside from the SDI problem, it is extremely difficult to achieve the kind of stabilizing reductions in nuclear forces that the United States seeks. This is because of the asymmetrical nuclear force structures (with the U.S.S.R. heavily dependent on ICBMs and the United States relatively more dependent on sea- and air-launched ballistic and cruise missiles), the projected Soviet gains in relative nuclear striking power with or without arms restrictions, and the new technical problems of verification (for example, the problem of verifying limits on mobile missiles and missiles with interchangeable conventional and nuclear warheads). Under these conditions the prospect for arms negotiations is stalemate.

The allies will tend to blame any failure of negotiations to produce agreement on President Reagan's refusal to use SDI as a bargaining chip unless Soviet intransigence is conspicuous. In time, if the U.S. position seems like a big obstacle to détente and arms control in Europe, the kind of popular and political protest that INF engendered (minus the on-site demonstrations) could be sparked. But as long as negotiations seem to be progressing (without sacrificing allied interests in Europe), this danger is in abeyance. In fact, the basic elements of a negotiable arms-control position that would satisfy allied as well as U.S. interests are fairly clear, although extremely difficult to translate into an actual agreement. In the summer of 1986 Moscow and Washington were apparently beginning to explore these elements with a mind to serious bargaining.

In the strategic forum the centerpiece of a negotiable position—the "grand bargain"—must be some kind of assurance to the Soviets that new or additional BMD would not be deployed or developed and tested beyond the restrictions of the ABM treaty for a number of years (both sides have spoken of ten) in return for the kind of reductions of strategic offensive warheads (particularly, the SS–18 warheads) that would decrease the vulnerability of U.S. ICBMs to a disarming first strike. In this kind of bargain the United States, by agreeing to adhere to the ABM treaty (which now has no time limit) for a period of years, or to extend the period of withdrawal from six months to several years, would nevertheless hope to keep alive the option of expanding BMD deployment. At the same time, the bargain would enhance the invulnerability of U.S. ICBMs at a substantially lower level of nuclear warheads without sacrificing any major opportunity to develop, test, or deploy segments of the SDI program, which are not likely to be ready for deployment until the 1990s in any case. In this way SDI would become a lever to achieve a more stable and advantageous strategic balance rather than an obstacle to an arms agreement or a bargaining chip to be given away.

However, it is doubtful that the Soviets will regard such a minimal restriction on SDI worth the price of reducing and restricting their ICBMs while enabling the United States to protect its own. Perhaps a more persuasive proposal would be to offer the Soviets a ten-year period of negotiations to revise the ABM treaty in order to permit expanded land-based BMD deployments that would protect counterforce targets, while extending the ABM treaty restrictions on space-based systems even further than ten years. Possibly, such a proposal not only would confront the Soviets with a more convincing implicit threat of unilateral strategic defensive deployments in the event that a revision of the ABM treaty was not reached; it might also draw a distinction between land-based and space-based BMD from which the Soviets would also derive some military gain, since they have already deployed ABMs around Moscow and are prepared to extend their deployment to other sites. To tighten further the restrictions against developing and testing components of space-based systems, the United States might also propose a limitation of ASATs to the two weapons systems already tested; such a limitation might be militarily beneficial because the United States depends more on military satellites, and its ASAT is superior.

Whatever the nature of a potential grand bargain, allied governments will be more interested in the prospect of achieving some agreement on strategic forces than in the precise terms of the agreement. The United States, in contrast, must be intensely concerned with the details. Obviously, it is easier to imagine the major elements of a grand bargain than to foresee the exact modalities, since the Soviets will want the greatest restrictions achievable for the least constraints on their strategic offensive programs and the Americans will seek just the opposite. If these differences are resolvable, they will be accommodated only after a protracted period of bargaining in which the allies will be anxious observers.

The opening gambits in strategic-force bargaining, set forth by the two heads of state in the summer of 1986, contained important differences on offensive as well as defensive restrictions, turning on the magnitude and categories of nuclear warhead reductions and the period and terms of commitment to observe the ABM treaty. These differences were not overcome at their dramatic October meeting in Reykjavik, where Reagan proposed the elimination of all offensive ballistic missiles in ten years, to be followed by SDI deployments unless the two sides agreed to extend the ABM treaty restrictions, and Gorbachev proposed to get rid of all strategic offensive weapons (including bombers and cruise missiles) in ten years, but not permit SDI deployments unless the two sides agreed to revise the ABM treaty. Arms control optimists believed that this exchange of utopias would impart new momentum toward agreement on the much more limited (approximately 30 percent) reductions that both sides proposed during a first-stage five-year period of negotiations and were encouraged by the concessions that both sides (but especially Gorbachev) made in their first-stage positions. Skeptics regarded Reykjavik principally as an improvised propaganda contest in which each side sought to capture the moral high ground in order to persuade the American and European publics of the justice of contradictory positions on SDI. In either case, if serious bargaining ensues, in the tough and protracted negotiations over the details, there will be no quick and sweeping resolution of the dozens of intractable issues that block the way to a mutually satisfactory and reliably verifiable military balance at a substantially reduced level of nuclear forces. And if an actual arms treaty results, it will probably be much closer to a freeze on existing deployments and programs than the kind of radical restructuring of the strategic balance that both sides talk about.

Subsidiary to the strategic negotiations but directly important to the allies are negotiations on theater nuclear weapons. From one standpoint an INF agreement should be much easier to reach, since the military significance of the numbers of these missiles is diminished by the existence of both shorter- and longer-range nuclear weapons that can strike European targets from inside or outside the theater, and since the theater balance is only a part of the global balance. But from another standpoint these facts suggest that the balance of nuclear weapons in the European theater cannot be resolved until the two sides have agreed on what the global balance should be. In any case, political objectives and calculations will be dominant in proposals to solve the military equation.

The dominance of political considerations—the contest for the hearts and minds of the European allies—was apparent in the two sides' opening INF proposals. In a five-year period the two sides agreed to eliminate all medium-range missiles in Europe, with some limits on medium-range missiles deployed in Soviet Asia and the United States, and then in a final stage to negotiate the elimination of remaining medium-range missiles and limits on short-range missiles. Even the U.S. first-stage (five-year) proposal—a reiteration of the "zero-zero" global elimination of medium-range missiles, which it had proposed in the heat of the INF crisis with the correct expectation that the Soviets would reject it—contained seeds of U.S.-allied controversy. It implicitly envisaged the unacceptable concept of a nonnuclear military balance, yet it would actually leave the Soviets with a large number of short-range and long-range missiles that could devastate Western Europe. Subsequent U.S. assurances that "collateral constraints" on Soviet short-range missiles would be included only partially met this concern.

In the month or two preceding the Reykjavik meeting the competitive exchange of utopias seemed to give way to preparations for serious bargaining as INF proposals shifted from the elimination of missiles to limiting them at reduced levels. Moscow's announcement that it would no longer link an INF agreement to its position on banning SDI and that it would no longer count the British and French nuclear forces as INF missiles encouraged Washington to believe that the outlines of an INF agreement might be quickly agreed. At Reykjavik, however, Gorbachev, after seeming to make concessions that converged with Reagan's proposals to create a combined INF and START (strategic arms reduction talk) agreement surpassing all previous expectations, insisted that any INF agreement would have to be part of the total package of arms agreements, which depended on U.S. acceptance of the restrictive Soviet terms of constraint on SDI research as well as development and testing.

European governments were clearly disturbed by President Reagan's eagerness to trade visions of the abolition of nuclear weapons (or at least of ballistic nuclear weapons) with the Soviets. His renewed proposal to eliminate all INF missiles in Europe was disturbing enough. They could barely suppress their relief at being saved by Gorbachev's reversal from confronting the unacceptable implications of Reykjavik for the nonnuclear defense of Europe and a credible U.S. deterrent. They were further reassured when, in mid-November 1986, President Reagan concurred with Prime Minister Thatcher that the "priority" in negotiations with the Soviet Union should be on seeking only a 50 percent cut in all strategic nuclear forces, a sharp reduction (but not elimination) of medium-range missiles, with restraints on short-range missiles, and a ban on chemical weapons, while taking steps toward eliminating Soviet advantages in nonnuclear forces.

If, as a result of these modifications of the U.S. arms-control position, the propaganda contest at Reykjavik gives way to serious bargaining at Geneva on the reduction of medium-range and long-range nuclear weapons, it will become obvious that the original U.S. concept of reaching the world of mutual assured defense and nuclear obsolescence by means of a ''cooperative transition'' is too ambitious a goal to be attainable and too radical a change in the structure of deterrence to be acceptable. This point is well understood by allied governments, although they diplomatically choose not to argue it. The goal of constructing a nuclear-free, defense-dominant structure is, on the one hand, too ambitious and incredible to attract the support of arms-control enthusiasts but, on the other hand, too linked with a vast military program to appeal to visionary nuclear abolitionists. Indeed, SDI, as President Reagan has presented it, is an odd marriage of a nuclear pacifist vision with an extraordinarily ambitious arms program, the first and most practical application of which will almost surely be the protection of military sites, not national populations. The irony is that, whereas the objective of countering nuclear strike forces with BMD might (at some stage when the technology has matured) be incorporated into a negotiable arms-control position that the allies could support, the goal of creating population shields presupposes a degree of Soviet cooperation and of multinational dependence on arms control that only the most ardent believers in disarmament believe possible.

Take the problem of verification alone. The Reagan administration has attached great weight to strict verification and compliance in its approach to existing and prospective treaties. For this administration to embrace a cooperative military structure that would have to be policed with a verification and compliance regime far more comprehensive, effective, and intrusive than any yet envisaged can only lend credence to the suspicion that SDI, no matter what the intentions of its founders, is in effect little more than a visionary sanction for engaging in a new phase of the arms competition for the sake of familiar security objectives.

Actually, these familiar security objectives—particularly, protecting retaliatory capabilities—evoke far less public opposition and more government acceptance in Europe than does SDI's visionary goal. But if strategic defense programs cannot be effectively related to compelling security needs and to a practical arms-control proposal for reducing nuclear warheads and making retaliatory forces less vulnerable, no revision of the ABM treaty is likely to be acceptable in Western Europe. U.S. abrogation of the treaty on the grounds of Soviet violation would be even less acceptable. Instead, the treaty seems destined to stand, in European as well as most American minds, as the indispensable and immutable protector of peace and security against dangerous new technological and industrial forces that are driving the arms race into space. Consequently, the vision of defensive shields may become the principal obstacle to obtaining a more stable mix of offensive and defensive weapons. This may be unfortunate from the long-run standpoint of Western military security, but it is a situation that the European allies greatly prefer to any alternative.

British and French Nuclear Forces

The British and French have a special reason for deploring SDI. Although not even the French wish to represent their opposition to SDI as a special national interest, they obviously do have such an interest: to preserve the utility of their independent nuclear forces. Their fear is that U.S. strategic defense deployments will lead to similar Soviet deployments, which will degrade the value of the independent nuclear forces in which the French and British have invested large funds for the highest political stakes.

The reasoning behind this view seems strained because it assumes (1) that the Soviet threat to the independent nuclear forces is only a function of the Soviet response to U.S. deployments, (2) that the United States will disregard the ABM treaty and reject any other arms restrictions in order to deploy strategic defense weapons to which the Soviets will respond in kind, (3) that these weapons will be deployed to protect cities, (4) that MIRVs and penetration aids will not enable British and French weapons to retain counter-city capabilities, and (5) that Soviet deployments will therefore provide such effective protection of cities as to negate the deterrent and political values the British and French now attribute to their independent forces. None of these assumptions is necessarily, or even probably, true. But it is understandable that the British and

French should assume the worst instead of the best outcome of uncertain scenarios based on a radically new structure of deterrence. Moreover, the British, at least, have reason to fear that the domestic opponents of an independent nuclear force will exploit the worst-case scenario to reinforce their case. And, as noted before, even French security experts argue that SDI may undermine the fragile domestic consensus supporting the whole range of French nuclear policies.

It is true that fulfillment of the ultimate SDI goal would entail the abolition of the British and French forces. Logically, there would be no reason for them if deterrence depended on conventional denial capabilities instead of nuclear punishment. But whatever loss of national prestige this novel situation would entail, it would at least have the advantage of relieving the allies of the anxieties and doubts that accompany their dependence on U.S. nuclear deterrence. Shifting the basis of deterrence in Europe from nuclear to conventional forces, moreover, might actually enhance the influence of British and French forces relative to U.S. forces by making the principal denomination of military power one in which the allies could be comparatively stronger. If the defensive military structure was only 70 percent instead of 100 percent effective, the equalizing tendency would be all the greater, on the assumption that all nuclear forces would be confined to a limited countercity function. If BMD deployments were restricted to protecting hard targets and if strategic offensive forces were greatly reduced, British and French forces might be sufficiently invulnerable to survive an attack but sufficiently lethal to penetrate residual urban defenses.

These speculations, however, are too fanciful or at least too conjectural to affect current European attitudes toward SDI. They pale into insignificance compared with the intuitive British and French feeling that an uncontrolled competition in strategic defense between the superpowers would depreciate the value of the weapons that have given them a claim to military independence in the nuclear age. In any case, such competition would greatly raise the expense and trouble of penetrating Soviet defenses.

To prevent the extension of East-West arms competition into antinuclear defense systems, the British and French rely on the ABM treaty. They will be particularly sensitive, therefore, to any signs of U.S. withdrawal from the treaty or of superpower revision of the treaty, unless it is in the context of a new comprehensive arms agreement that protects the British and French independent nuclear forces while reducing the level of superpower forces. Only in that context, moreover, would they consider a proportionate reduction of their own forces.

The Soviets, however, in their proposals for arms reductions, initially sought to link the British and French nuclear forces to INF, whereas the British and French consistently refused to negotiate any limits on their forces in the INF context on the ground that they are independent *strategic* forces. During the deployment crisis the Soviets proposed reductions of INF down to numbers of missiles equivalent to the British and French numbers, thereby, in effect, calling on the United States to count the British and French forces against theater weapons while reducing INF forces to zero. After the deployment of Pershing IIs and cruise missiles began, the Soviets made the reduction of SS–20s and INFs contingent on banning SDI—a requirement that was obviously unacceptable to the United States. Then, in an apparent concession, the Soviets proposed that, in the initial stage of eliminating all nuclear weapons, medium-range missiles in the European theater (but not in Asia) should be reduced to zero *without* requiring a ban on SDI. While separating INF from SDI, however, the Soviets made the proposed reductions contingent on freezing the British and French forces, which are scheduled to be augmented by about 1,200 warheads through MIRVs, and on prohibiting the transfer of U.S. technology to these forces. Because the British and French would reduce their forces only in conjunction with strategic nuclear reductions by the superpowers and because the Soviets evidently will not agree to such reductions without constraints on SDI that are stricter even than the U.S. restrictive interpretation of the ABM treaty, the effect of their proposal was not to facilitate an agreement on theater nuclear weapons but only to put the onus on the British and French for blocking an INF agreement. At the same time, the Soviets retained the option of presenting SDI to the allies as the major obstacle to achieving nuclear arms reductions in Europe.

Then, in the fall of 1986, the Soviets seemed to be considering concessions that could lead to an INF agreement long before an agreement on strategic offensive weapons could be reached. They indicated that they no longer regarded British and French nuclear forces as medium-range missiles that must be counted in INF limitations. If subsequent talks and bargaining had confirmed these indications, this would have signaled Soviet eagerness for a reasonable INF agreement, although it would still have left the problem of adjusting the reduction and limitation of British and French forces to strategic force arms reductions. Gorbachev's repackaging of any INF agreement as part of a comprehensive agreement conditioned on SDI restrictions unacceptable to the United States ended any such prospect, at least for the next round of arms talks. For the British and French governments this was a relief. But the Thatcher government could hardly ignore the encouragement that the failure of arms control might offer to the Labour party, which is committed to unilateral British nuclear disarmament.

SDI's Implications for Defense Expenditures

As the limits of SDI and the remoteness and unlikelihood of the achievement of its ultimate goal become apparent, allied concerns tend to focus on more proximate issues and choices. One of these concerns is SDI's implications for defense expenditures.

Allied governments expect a program funded on the immense scale of SDI to gather political and bureaucratic momentum and powerful sponsors. Whatever its tangible military results, they believe SDI, as a multifaceted weapons program, is here to stay. Some members of the European defense community worry that the resulting expenditures and the human and material resources they consume will be a diversion of funds from higher-priority needs, such as strengthening conventional defense capabilities on NATO's central front. The supreme allied commander in Europe, General Bernard Rogers, has loudly lent his voice to this view. This apprehension is part of a larger concern that springs from the fact that allied governments are being urged—and most of them now agree with the proposed goal, in principle—to raise NATO's nuclear threshold with strengthened conventional capabilities, including costly deep-attack missiles and C³I technology, at a time in which budget austerity and high rates of unemployment virtually preclude increased defense expenditures.

SDI as a Technological Enterprise

The other side of the concerns the NATO allies have expressed about the adverse impact of SDI on defense expenditures is their desire to share the benefits of high-technology enterprise that the immense investments in SDI research are presumed to offer. As of now the economic desire far outweighs the economic apprehension in its influence on European positions on SDI. Reconciled to the fact that the SDI program is here to stay, most European government and industry leaders are disposed to get aboard the train of technological bounties before it leaves the station. Although the European share of contracts may be disappointing, European industries can at least look forward to gaining access to technological know-how.

This disposition toward participation is reinforced by the concern that Western Europe, afflicted with structural deficiencies that impede its competitiveness in modern high-technological enterprise, is in danger of forfeiting to the United States and Japan the economic benefits of the new technological boom, while suffering a brain drain of its best scientists to U.S. corporations. Already painfully impressed by U.S. dominance of the high-technology military marketplace and resentful of the U.S. failure to establish a true two-way street in military procurement and trade, European governments and entrepreneurs are all the more determined to get a fair share of SDI technology, with its promise of civilian spinoffs.

The U.S. government, conscious of these European feelings and sensing an opportunity to elicit European support of at least one aspect of SDI, has encouraged European governments and industries to join the United States in this vast research program. General James Abrahamson, head of the SDI organization in the Pentagon, has forecast significant civilian spinoffs and formed the Office of Education and Civil Applications to foster them. This facet of SDI began with Defense Secretary Caspar Weinberger's personal initiative of March 1985, inviting the allies to join SDI research. It was followed by a memorandum of understanding with Britain in December outlining the research areas and the principles and structure for managing technological participation, which cleared the way for a similar agreement in March 1986 with West Germany, notwithstanding the opposition of the Social Democratic party and

Foreign Minister Hans-Dietrich Genscher on political grounds and the opposition of Finance Minister Gerhard Stoltenberg on financial grounds. This agreement, in turn, assures an agreement with Italy. (U.S. officials have said they expect similar agreements with Israel and Japan.)

However, France has taken the lead in opposing such official participation in SDI. In the name of independent European cooperation it has tried to organize a European surrogate based on a Franco-German foundation. Efforts supported by Great Britain and West Germany to organize the collective participation of British, West German, French, and Italian companies in SDI failed at the economic summit in Bonn in May 1985. This failure left European countries free to participate in an independent counterpart to SDI, which could be the means of competing for SDI contracts more competitively or of generating exclusively European enterprises. Predictably, France seized this opportunity.

The French government, whose officials were initially the most outspoken critics of SDI, rejected government-to-government participation. Instead, it proposed in April 1985 an ostensibly non-military cooperative high-technology program, Eureka (European Research Coordination Agency). Eureka—a loosely organized, open-ended association intended to attract industrial participation and investment—is supposed to give European countries, and West Germany in particular, a multinational civilian alternative to SDI research (although, in fact, most of the projects envisaged are dual-use, that is, military and commercial). Nevertheless, France gave the green light to its government-owned electronics and weapons companies, notably Matra and Thomson, to compete for SDI contracts. Although President Mitterrand continued to oppose French participation on grounds of national independence, Prime Minister Chirac, whose conservative coalition gained him a power-sharing role in the parliamentary elections of March 1986, took the position that France could not afford to remain aloof from SDI research.

At the same time, there was a growing sentiment among French political and industrial leaders that France should follow the U.S. example and develop its own space-defense program, independently or with European cooperation. The goal was not to gain perfect protection for the nation but to enhance deterrence by countering Soviet offensive missiles, including the SS-20. To give this goal a European dimension the Mitterrand government presented it as part of a European Defense Initiative (EDI) and explored, within the framework of emerging Franco-German defense cooperation, collaborative programs with West Germany, which expressed interest in developing a European shield against cruise missiles and short-range nuclear missiles.

This prospect has attracted considerable German interest in a general way. German Defense Minister Manfred Worner has welcomed French cooperation in developing an ATBM, although he has proposed undertaking this cooperation in the context of a revitalized Western European Union (WEU) in order to assure its compatibility with the Federal Republic's commitment to NATO. Former chancellor Helmut Schmidt, in a notable speech in the Bundestag (on June 28, 1984), called for a joint Franco-German industrial program, an expanded Franco-German conventional defense effort, and a French nuclear guarantee to cover West German territory. In April 1984, Jurgen Todenhofer, a conservative party spokesman on defense matters, went a step further toward Franco-German military collaboration but put it in a transatlantic framework, when he proposed the creation of an integrated U.S.-European nuclear force that would include the Federal Republic. But none of these schemes for a new framework of Franco-German military cooperation has received official endorsement, and France is clearly opposed to any kind of nuclear or, by logical extension, antinuclear weapons cooperation, whether bilateral or multilateral.

Consequently, whether Eureka and EDI can provide the best of three worlds—a competitive European surrogate for SDI, along with an independent French program and unofficial industrial participation in the U.S. program—is problematical. In June 1985 the four largest European electronics companies—Siemens, Philips, General Electric, and Thomson—signed a statement of intent to cooperate on several different projects within the framework of Eureka. Some contracts have been signed. But the British, notwithstanding successful collaboration with the French on the Airbus and the Arianne space launcher, are drawn more toward cooperation with the United States than with France. West Germany is ambivalent. It must preserve its strong U.S. ties in all security matters. It also badly wants closer French cooperation; but the French have given no tangible signs of willingness to extend such cooperation to the nuclear level, and no Germans believe that French cooperation could in any way be a substitute for the U.S. connection. Under these circumstances, the German government is afraid that the exclusivist bias of Eureka, in combination with U.S. pressure to join SDI research, will jeopardize one or both of its security ties. At the same time, it must heed strong domestic opposition from the Social Democratic party (SPD) against participation in either a European or a U.S. military program associated with SDI.

As things now stand, in spite of political opposition to SDI in the German Social Democratic and the British Labour parties, all the *major* European governments except France have accepted (or, in the case of Italy, probably will soon accept) official participation in SDI research. Concomitantly, allied governments have muted their overt criticism of SDI's strategic implications and emphasized the necessity of SDI research for developing hard-point defense and for gaining civilian as well as military technological spinoffs. In this way, SDI as a technological enterprise has enabled most of the allies to reconcile the program with allied solidarity—particularly, for the sake of good relations with the United States but also out of reluctance to lend credence to the Soviet campaign to muster European opposition to SDI.

Nevertheless, there is considerable and well-founded skepticism in Europe (1) that the United States will award the most lucrative contracts to European instead of U.S. companies; (2) that the European share of contracts for weapons systems and major components, as opposed to subcontracts, will be more than a token; and (3) that the U.S. government, considering its emphasis on preventing the leak of critical technologies to the East, will share the most advanced technologies with Europe. Some Europeans estimate that only about 1 percent of the total contracted funds will go to European companies.

Europeans, however, have learned to live with their skepticism about the extent of U.S. commercial and financial cooperation while making the most of it for the sake of the overriding benefits of security cooperation. European governments and industries are already prepared for a meager share of SDI by the sparse benefits derived from the highly touted emerging technology program. In the end, Europe's share will probably be satisfying if not entirely satisfactory, providing that U.S. funding does not decline too far from the official projections of up to $60 billion over the next ten years. But unless European industries, whether through Eureka or otherwise, can combine their resources in an economically efficient way to overcome the artificially fragmented European market, they are likely to remain very junior partners in the production of SDI-related technology.

European accommodation to SDI as a technological enterprise, in any case, does not mean European approval of SDI as a U.S. military program to restructure deterrence. The allies have accepted SDI as a research program and, perhaps, as a technological resource that might some day protect European military sites but not as a test of loyalty to President Reagan's vision, which they profoundly oppose. Any efforts on the part of the Reagan administration to convey the notion that an endorsement of SDI as a technological enterprise is a vote for SDI as a whole can only play into the hands of SDI's opponents and give the Soviets a major talking point.

Antitactical Ballistic Missiles

As the various facets of SDI materialize, there is one kind of weapon in the vast array of antinuclear defensive weapons technologies that is likely to have special significance for European military security, although it was not originally envisaged as part of a multilayered defense system: ATBMs. The ATBM category could encompass a variety of missiles with conventional warheads, theoretically capable of intercepting and destroying incoming ballistic and cruise missiles of "tactical" rather than "strategic" range (and, therefore, not prohibited by the ABM treaty as long as they have not been tested in an ABM mode and do not use components transferred from ABMs). Some have already been developed. Improvements through further research and development are likely to give them a useful military role in defending military targets on land in the European theater long before a useful system of layered defense to protect national populations in the United States or the Soviet Union could be developed, let alone deployed as a cost-effective and affordable system. Against the SS–20, with its exo-atmospheric trajectory, longer-range BMD would be required in order to distinguish armed warheads from decoys in midcourse as part of a layered defense (although the lower payload of the SS-20 would leave less room for decoys than would be the case with long-range missiles). But against the so-called short-range INF (SS-21, SS-22, and SS-23)—accurate dual-capable missiles with ranges of 75, 550, and 300 miles, respectively—ATBMs would be appropriate because the problem of effective terminal interceptors is simplified by the slower velocity and the largely or entirely atmospheric trajectory.

As an outgrowth of their surface-to-air missile technology, the Soviets have already developed and tested and are in the process of deploying at least one first-generation ATBM: the mobile SAX-12. (U.S. officials do not credit the anticruise missile SA-10 with an ATBM capability, although it might be upgraded for this purpose.) At the current rate of development, Soviet ATBMs, working together with improved ABMs, will give the Soviets a significant terminal-defense capability in Europe before the year 2000. The United States, in contrast, has no deployable ATBM. The likeliest candidate is the surface-to-surface Patriot, but the Patriot would have to be redesigned with new sensors and a C³I network in order to acquire a useful ATBM capability; and even then, according to some sources, it would be very expensive and of marginal utility with a conventional warhead, which is politically indispensable. Other candidates—for example, the army's low altitude defense system (LoADS) or small radar hypersonic homing intercept (SR Hit)—may be more promising but would also have to be adapted to ATBM requirements.

The potential military significance of ATBMs arises most directly from their relevance to trends in strategy and forces in the European theater since the late 1960s, particularly the Soviet emphasis on an initial, conventional blitzkrieg option, combined with the proliferation of mobile nuclear and nonnuclear strike missiles. Both options are intended to nullify NATO's nuclear first-use option while overwhelming its minimal conventional defense capability. Soviet ATBMs can contribute to Soviet theater capabilities by countering INF and by protecting the Soviets' enormous and increasing lead in nuclear warheads deliverable on theater targets. This lead results from large and continuing SS-20 deployments (at the end of 1985, 441 launchers with three warheads each), the initial deployments of the SS-21s, SS-22s, and SS-23s, added to the older longer-range SS–11s and SS–9s, and the greatly expanded force of Soviet theater nuclear aircraft. No less significant in the long run may be the role of ATBMs in protecting the Soviets' new generation of deep-interdiction missiles with conventional warheads, part of a burgeoning Soviet emerging technology program.

From the U.S. standpoint the principal military role of ATBMs would be to diminish the great and growing vulnerability of concentrations of general purpose forces and critical military targets in Western Europe, including air and missile bases, to Soviet ballistic and cruise missiles. The overriding objective of protecting these targets would be to strengthen the implementation of the conventional and the limited nuclear options postulated in the 1967 NATO doctrine of flexible and controlled response (MC 14/3), by denying the Soviets a decisive first-strike capability and enhancing the survival of INF and other retaliatory forces.

The principal political objective of ATBM deployments would be to enhance the credibility of an effective conventional response to a conventional attack, demonstrate the commitment of U.S. SDI efforts to the defense of Europe, validate the U.S. commitment to provide equal protection for the allies as a counterpart to SDI, and counter any diversion of Soviet targeting from U.S. to European targets that might result from extended ABM or other SDI deployments in the United States. The validity of these objectives is reinforced by evidence of an independent European interest in ATBMs. Some British and French defense experts and officials regard ATBMs as an attractive means of protecting their independent nuclear forces. German defense officials and politicians have expressed interest in ATBMs to counter Soviet cruise missiles and short-range nuclear missiles. French and German spokesmen have indicated that the European allies might develop their own ATBM, perhaps with U.S. assistance, as part of a transatlantic division of labor. This collective project would give the allies the technological benefits of a major weapon system directly related to their own security, as opposed to mere subcontracts in the SDI program.

Indeed, the U.S. government, in its preoccupation with its own problem of ICBM vulnerability, may have initially underestimated the political allure of ATBMs in Europe, just as it underestimated both the allure of INF in Europe and the opposition to it. The political dividends of ATBMs are foreshadowed in the growing interest in ATBMs among allied defense specialists, especially in West Germany, where Defense Minister Manfred Worner has explicitly advocated them, and in France, where official spokesmen have advocated developing a European ATBM as well as a space-based defense system.

This enthusiasm, however, may be based more on political hopes than technological and economic realities. At a time of declining expenditures on conventional forces allied governments are unlikely to launch an expensive ATBM development program, and the United States is unlikely to subsidize such a program. Furthermore, U.S. promotion of ATBMs, in response to official European requests, could, like U.S. sponsorship of INF, provoke a popular opposition to deployments that would turn a political dividend into a political crisis. The reason is that ATBMs, because they are closely related to ABMs and other strategic defense weapons and because they would be visible targets for antinuclear demonstrators, not only raise questions of technological and economic feasibility but also raise potentially explosive political issues in domestic politics and East-West relations.

One issue arises because of the ambiguity of the distinction between ABMs and ATBMs. The technology of some ATBMs is not much different from that of ABMs. ATBMs—the SAX–12 is an example—could be given an ABM range and function. The ambiguity of range is illustrated by the fact that some technically nonstrategic offensive missiles (like the SS–20) and bombers (like the Soviet Backfire) already have ranges that can reach U.S. strategic targets. Politically, this ambiguity cuts both ways. On the one hand, the similarity of ATBMs to ABMs might take some of the political onus off land-based SDI and help to link U.S. strategic defense to European tactical defense. And the development and deployment of ATBMs in Europe might even make it easier to revise the ABM treaty to permit extended ABM deployments. On the other hand, the development and deployment of ATBMs will probably be regarded by antimilitary parties and groups in Europe as a dangerous circumvention of the ABM treaty and a stalking horse for SDI. (With this in mind, the Soviets deny that they have an ATBM and warn that any Western effort to develop one would be contrary to the ABM treaty.) ATBMs will also be condemned in these quarters as contributions to a warfighting strategy, which will raise the likelihood of a catastrophic war on European soil.

Such public opposition to ATBMs might also raise the contentious issue of an ATBM ban or limitation to prevent an arms race in Europe between offensive and defensive weapons, especially if an INF arms agreement is reached or seems likely. In the short run, the Soviet advantage in ATBM development may be an argument for seeking an ATBM ban, perhaps in the context of a tightening of the ABM treaty's restrictions; but in the longer run NATO's great vulnerability to Soviet nuclear weapons and the general trend toward converting theater nuclear forces into conventional forces argues for investing in ATBMs as part of a badly needed effort to strengthen air defense in Western Europe. In any case, a ban or moratorium would freeze a Soviet advantage in ATBMs at this stage of Western underdevelopment of the technology.

ATBMs also raise a military operational issue with significant political overtones because of the potential complementary role of SDI weapons, whether based in space or on land. To counter SS–20s and Soviet intermediate-range ballistic missiles (IRBMs) and ICBMs that could be targeted against Western Europe, ABMs and some space-based systems would be necessary complements to ATBMs in defending NATO military targets. If the United States deploys or contemplates deploying BMDs for the protection of its own military targets, whether by means of a revised ABM treaty or otherwise, it will have a strong political incentive to extend SDI coverage to its European allies, if only to assuage their fears of decoupling, which the Soviets would be eager to exploit. But a multilayered defense system, in addition to entailing immense technical problems and great expense, would be even more politically provocative than ATBMs.

The United States will also have a military incentive, going beyond NATO security objectives, to extend SDI coverage to Europe. The space-based sensors and C³I equipment necessary to protect the United States will also provide the European theater with major defensive spinoffs. Employing these spinoffs to deter or blunt a Soviet attack on Europe may seem like a way to prevent the extension of a war to the United States and may hedge against the Soviet enhancement of IRBM ranges to saturate strategic defense weapons protecting the United States. However, the technical problems of integrating BMD with ATBM (for example, the problem of adequate battle management sensors and computers) would be immense.

Some of the political implications of this military logic are worrisome, but under some conditions SDI might also be turned to political advantage. Whatever may be the military case for linking SDI to the defense of Western Europe, the political effect might be to arouse public opinion in Europe against absorption into an allegedly provocative U.S. SDI program. However, if SDI can be dissociated from either a strategy of population defense or war fighting and if SDI can also be integrated into an arms-control position that the allies can identify with their special interests and perspectives, its extension to Europe and its linkage to ATBMs might be a political asset. A revision of the ABM treaty might facilitate such an integration of SDI into an arms limitation by permitting expanded land-based terminal defense deployments and banning the testing and deployment of space-based systems for a period of years. In the context of an agreement on offensive warhead reductions, this revision would also provide the basis for the limitation of other nuclear weapons in Europe at reduced levels. It might also provide the basis for clarifying the distinction between ATBMs and ABMs in order to prevent a divisive conflict on this question in European domestic politics.

Of course, such speculations about the military and political significance of ATBMs are inconclusive until much more is known about the technology (which can never be tested under realistic battle conditions) and its cost (which is bound to be immense and perhaps not cost-effective, compared with a combination of passive defense and counterforce measures to achieve the same military objectives). Nevertheless, it is possible that if the Soviet ATBM program continues to progress at the same pace, this development, added to the large conventional and nuclear advantage the Soviets have already attained in the European theater, could affect the fate of SDI at least as much as the vulnerability of the land-based leg of the U.S. strategic triad. In any case, the emergence of ATBM issues seems likely to be one of several factors that will turn European and U.S. SDI concerns increasingly toward terminal defense of land-based targets intended to enhance the existing basis of direct and extended deterrence, while the goal of population shields recedes into the background as a dramatic expression of the inveterate longing to escape the nuclear dilemma.

THE FUTURE

Judging from the course of SDI in transatlantic relations thus far, SDI appears likely to remain a source of consternation among Europe's political and military leaders. However, the widespread opposition to its ultimate goal among defense specialists probably will be subordinated to the avoidance of transatlantic dissension and a desire to reap the benefits of technological enterprise. Therefore, SDI does not seem likely to trigger the kind of popular opposition that INF did or to disrupt the relatively harmonious state of transatlantic relations since the INF crisis. SDI might even contribute to this harmony if it seems to be a lever for progress in arms control, a source of technological enrichment, and a program from which ATBM technology relevant to the conventional defense of Europe can be derived. However, this judgment is contingent on three questionable conditions: (1) that SDI remains a research program rather than a program of developing, testing, or deploying BMD beyond the restrictive interpretation of the ABM treaty; (2) that holding open the option of such a BMD deployment seems compatible with fruitful arms negotiations and an eventual arms agreement that will stabilize nuclear deterrence at a lower level of forces; and (3) that the prospect of expanded BMD deployments in the United States is compatible with European wishes for equal protection without provocation.

A number of developments might contravene these conditions and serve as catalysts for crisis:

1. Because SDI is a research program aimed at deployment, sooner or later the decision of whether to test and deploy SDI weapons will arise. A positive decision could raise and amplify all the strategic, operational, military, and arms-control issues that were foreshadowed in the initial alarms touched off by President Reagan's proclamation. These issues would be brought to a head if they entailed U.S. abrogation of or withdrawal from the ABM treaty rather than its agreed revision. If U.S. deployment of BMDs leads to the deployment of SDI weapons *in* Europe or even only

over Europe (that is, the sensors and satellites serving U.S.-based BMD), SDI could become a matter of public controversy and of INF-like tensions between the United States and its allies. Unlike the INF crisis, an SDI or SDI-ATBM crisis might mobilize European governments as well as the antinuclear activists against U.S. policies.

2. The most likely reason the United States might decide to deploy SDI before the end of this century would be to protect its land-based missiles and C³I because there appeared to be no other politically as well as technologically and economically feasible way to rescue a survivable land-based ICBM force in the face of a growing Soviet advantage in hard-target-kill ICBMs. The impact of this deployment decision on U.S.-allied relations would depend, among other things, on whether projected deployments were confined to ABMs rather than extended to space-based weapons and whether they were made cooperatively by revision of the ABM treaty instead of unilaterally in defiance of the treaty. If neither of the latter conditions obtained, U.S. BMD deployments could lead to a major transatlantic crisis.

3. In the next couple of decades the infusion of ATBM competition into the East-West military confrontation in Europe, along with the conversion of many tactical and perhaps some strategic functions from nuclear to conventional weapons, could so cloud the distinction between ATBMs and ABMs and between the roles of nuclear and conventional missiles as to make the strategic rationale of the ABM treaty—crisis stability through the severe limitation of defense against missiles and the unalterable vulnerability of nations to nuclear devastation—obsolete. Just the Soviet deployment of mobile ATBMs—integrated with ABMs upgradable to ABM ranges and assigned to protect military targets enmeshed with urban centers—could obliterate the distinctions on which the treaty's restrictions were based. The politically troublesome question of whether to revise or abandon the ABM treaty may therefore arise before long. Whether the deployment of ATBMs would facilitate or obstruct the revision of the ABM treaty will depend on a number of factors, not the least of which is the official U.S. rationale for SDI and the way the United States relates SDI to strategic arms reductions. But, unless the treaty is revised in East-West agreement, the proliferation of ATBMs and the conversion of nuclear to

conventional functions would almost surely make the ABM treaty the focal point of a divisive transatlantic strategic debate. This debate may be foreshadowed in the issues raised by the very prospect of ATBM development, testing, and deployment before the end of this century. The debate would be complicated by the achievement, or just the lively prospect of the achievement, of an INF reduction and limitation, since ATBMs would then seem all the greater threat to the military balance that an INF agreement was supposed to stabilize.

4. Although the United States may continue to adhere to the ABM treaty while seeking reductions of SS–18s and other Soviet ICBMs, the Soviets might, at some point, reach the conclusion that their effort to curb the SDI program through public diplomacy and arms control had failed and decide to deploy a full-scale, nation-wide BMD system in a sudden "breakout" or perhaps a "creep-out," on the grounds that the United States had rejected all reasonable arms-control proposals and was preparing to seek stra-tegic superiority through SDI deployments. Or the Soviets might threaten to do this in order to strengthen their leverage for special restrictions on ASATs and space-based BMD development and testing. The first course would compel the United States to respond with offensive and defensive measures. If the Soviet breakout or creep-out was confined to land-based systems, the United States would have to choose whether to respond with the full range of layered-defense weapons or with only a reciprocally limited land-based program. A Soviet threat of breakout as a bargaining lever would compel the United States to choose among making a sim-ple counterthreat, accepting the Soviet arms-control position, or proposing some other alternative.

5. The Soviets, unable to stop the U.S. program aimed at space-based deployments, might propose an arms agreement to permit extended land-based ABM deployments but ban space-based deployments while reducing the number of offensive nuclear warheads on terms that would give the Soviets a strategic advan-tage (for example, by permitting mobile ICBMs with MIRVs) and leave the European allies vulnerable (for example, by banning ABMs in Europe). The United States would then have to face, in the con-text of arms negotiations foreshadowing superpower collusion, the potentially disruptive SDI issues that spring from the differential

vulnerability of Europe. The United States might also face the heightened prospect of a Soviet ABM breakout if it rejected Soviet terms. Nevertheless, the United States might well turn a Soviet proposal to revise the ABM treaty to its advantage if it was prepared to incorporate a limited extension of ABM deployments into the grand arms bargain entailing deep reductions in offensive missiles and bombers that many supporters as well as opponents of SDI have proposed.

6. If the Soviets maintain their present negotiating tactics, as seems likely for at least the next several years, and the U.S. government (even after the Reagan administration) both adheres to the ABM treaty and rejects any additional restrictions on space-based SDI as a bargaining lever, the Soviets may succeed in convincing European countries and their publics (and important segments of the U.S. Congress, too) that U.S. insistence on pursuing population shields to make nuclear deterrence obsolete is the principal obstacle to strategic reductions. If the Soviets simultaneously manage to offer nuclear force reductions, a complete ban on testing of nuclear weapons, and other proposals that are irresistibly attractive to European publics (and to Left-leaning governments, if they should replace the present conservative ones), European opposition to SDI might give the Soviets a better wedge to drive between the United States and its allies than INF turned out to be. Alternatively, the Soviets might accept such deep reductions of SS–18 missiles that the United States could not refuse a ten- or fifteen-year ban on SDI development, testing, and deployment, which, after President Reagan is out of office, might be tantamount to a permanent ban.

7. A Labour party victory in Great Britain and, less likely, an SPD return to power in West Germany would strengthen antimilitary forces throughout Western Europe and would greatly enhance the influence on governments of the Soviet campaign to represent SDI and any related Western military program as the sole obstacle to disarmament and détente.

8. If, contrary to present indications, deep reductions or the elimination of whole classes of nuclear weapons are reached in a comprehensive East-West agreement, without unacceptable (from the American standpoint) restrictions on SDI development and testing or against future SDI deployments, European opposition to

any strategic or tactical defense programs that are inconsistent with a restrictive interpretation of the ABM treaty would be greatly strengthened. But, simultaneously, the United States might be plunged into a vociferous BMD debate, or the U.S. government might be engaged in a desperate campaign against European (and probably congressional) opposition to keep alive the SDI options technically permitted by the postulated arms agreement. The divisive effect upon U.S.-European relations could be greater than any effect of strategic differences in the absence of a treaty.

None of these developments is inevitable or necessarily the stuff of crisis if it should occur. All of these developments can be either prevented or managed. Some might be turned to the benefit of NATO. But any of them could seriously aggravate rather than mitigate the dilemma of Europe's nuclear dependence if SDI is not approached in the context of an integrated defense and arms-control policy that reconciles U.S. and European perspectives, as outlined in this chapter.

The wisest policies, however, will not entirely solve Europe's nuclear dilemma, which any major change in NATO's military posture or strategy—and certainly the changes inherent in SDI—is bound to accentuate. The beginning of wisdom is to accept this fact as long as NATO serves its central purposes. Instinctively, the allied governments do accept the dilemma. Sooner or later, visions of population shields notwithstanding, it will become evident that the U.S. government also accepts the dilemma as unavoidable. Only on this basis can the allies effectively cope with the practical policy issues of applying the new BMD technology toward reducing NATO's dependence on nuclear retaliation. Without the disruptive distraction of antinuclear shields, NATO may gradually assimilate the practical elements of SDI to the endless task of alleviating its nuclear dilemma rather than strain its fabric of cohesion in a futile effort to abolish the dilemma. Military assimilation presupposes the continuing political adaptation of the requirements of transatlantic collaboration to the European allies' search for a greater measure of control over their collective security, but that is a subject beyond the scope of this chapter.

4.
SDI, EUROPE, AND THE AMERICAN STRATEGIC DILEMMA

David P. Calleo

Many Europeans look upon SDI as a strange religious frenzy that has somehow overtaken their distant imperial court. Cast in the role of conservative provincials, they have had trouble grasping the new faith. They have been able neither to figure out what President Reagan's vision was meant to be nor to develop any clear idea about what it is likely to become. As first revealed, the president's program seemed designed to make nuclear deterrence obsolete. Authoritative disciples soon described it as an enhancement of deterrence.[1] Reading between the lines, Europeans thought SDI might be primarily a bargaining chip for forcing the Soviets into an arms agreement. Or they saw it as another great technological boondoggle to keep the United States' scientific and strategic communities well provisioned beyond the end of the century.

Even if the program's original intent had been crystal clear, great uncertainties about its likely evolution would still exist. The president's continental bubble to cover American cities would require space-based weapons, which, even if they could be developed, would remain highly vulnerable to preemptive attack.[2] Such a defensive regime, to be stable, would appear to require so intense a degree of cooperation between the superpowers as to constitute a sort of world government, a project that would seem highly fanciful even if among the Western allies, let alone between rival superpowers. If the bubble is almost certainly infeasible for the United States, as nearly everyone except the president apparently concedes, it seems absolutely impossible for Western Europe.[3] Since Russia is, after all, part of Europe, there seems to be no remotely conceivable technology to insulate West European territory from Soviet missiles, let alone other means of nuclear and conventional attack.

A more limited ballistic missile defense (BMD) for "point" defense—to cover such targets as U.S. missiles, command centers, bases, and even specific cities—is more feasible technically and could also be deployed to cover similar targets in Europe. Several studies believe point defense of missiles could be effective strategically, particularly if combined with mobile and deceptive basing, because any preemptive attack might well have to use up many more missiles than the attacker could expect to destroy on the ground. But many other studies suggest that point defense, even for missile sites, would be either unnecessary, because of the great diversity of U.S. retaliatory capabilities, or not cost-effective, because such a defense would cost more overall to develop and install than the additional or adapted offensive missiles required to overwhelm it.[4] Moreover, the Russians, with an ample supply of heavy missiles, are particularly well fixed to increase their number of warheads drastically. Under the circumstances many Americans find it hard to see any national advantage in taking the lead to deploy such weapons. Europeans, with their additional geographical disadvantages, seem even less-favorably situated for deployment.

Insofar as BMD could be effective, many analysts worry about its possible destabilizing consequences. If only one superpower achieved an operative space-based bubble, it would have achieved strategic hegemony. The other might feel compelled to strike before such a system could be deployed. If both had bubbles, total victory would follow from a successful strike against the space bases of the other. More plausibly, a superpower well-endowed with point missile defenses might strike first on the grounds that its own BMD could easily contain whatever retaliatory force remained to the opponent.[5] Each side, fearful of being disarmed by a first strike, would feel compelled to strike first to preempt. Many American analysts wonder if it will ever make sense to initiate deployments that will result in such mutually unfavorable circumstances. Many Europeans agree.

Low expectations for SDI have begun to extend even to SDI's diplomatic usefulness. Europeans applauded SDI's apparent role in bringing the Soviets back to arms talks. They keep hoping that Reagan's subsequent unwillingness to negotiate over SDI is games-manship rather than obduracy. As time goes on, the hope proves difficult to sustain without more positive reinforcement than it has yet received. Europeans have begun to suspect that even if the Americans never deploy SDI, they will prove incapable of parlay-ing it into a serious arms agreement.

Europeans were immediately impressed by the possibilities of SDI as an industrial boondoggle. The scale of the proposed research funding seemed highly promising for the branches of science and technology involved. European firms have feared the spinoff would greatly favor their American industrial rivals and have therefore been eager to pick up whatever business—and information—they can get. The Pentagon has vigorously promoted sanguine expec-tations. Past and recent experience, however, has discouraged any excessive or unguarded optimism about sharing in U.S. military research and procurement. After years of wrangling over Eastern trade and technology transfer, Europeans have grown attentive to the pitfalls of cooperation.[6]

Europeans have now had over three years to wrestle with what SDI means for them. As they now see it, any actual program is like-ly to be far less disturbing than the initial rhetoric. As they look at the manifold strategic risks and ambiguities, the preposterous costs and the manifest disagreements within the American political and strategic communities, including the Reagan administration itself, they cannot make themselves believe that SDI will ever fulfill either Reagan's revolutionary hopes or their own corresponding fears.

Europeans, to be sure, may be allowing their particular interests to cloud their general judgment. Their own military interests strongly predispose them against heavy superpower investment in missile defense. Defensive systems might have a disproportionately weighty effect on Europe's own nuclear deterrents. The upgrading planned for British and French nuclear forces by the mid-1990s might, in theory, be robbed of much of its effectiveness. The French have declared themselves confident about their ability to penetrate missile defenses with modified and more numerous warheads.[7] But the French cannot be enthusiastic about the resources this will take—resources to be wrested from the civilian sector or, more probably, from other parts of their military budget. Depleting conventional arms, including normal air defense, may reduce security overall. Europe is, after all, highly vulnerable to nonballistic air attack, not to mention the Red Army's tanks.[8]

Europeans also fear SDI's effects on the U.S. military budget. The French problem with budgets is a miniature version of the American. If SDI proceeds to even limited deployment, a vast sum will have to be attracted away from a combination of U.S. civilian and other military programs.[9] Given the current state of U.S. budgetary politics, other military programs are likely to be a prime source. Particularly vulnerable will be the large, very expensive conventional forces the United States justifies chiefly by their role in the defense of Western Europe. Since up to half the U.S. defense budget can be attributed to such forces, SDI is likely to make the long-gestating American inclination to withdraw conventional forces from Europe increasingly difficult to resist.[10] A substantial diminishing of U.S. forces for NATO that leads to a notable improvement in the American fiscal situation could have substantial compensating benefits for Europe, particularly if a significant Europeanization of the alliance was the result. In due course, a reduced U.S. fiscal deficit could certainly have highly beneficial long-term effects for the world economy. But SDI seems an unlikely way to lower the U.S. military budget and fiscal deficit, even if it does reduce the American conventional commitment to Europe.

Many Europeans, of course, fear that the urge to "decouple" from the risks of extended nuclear deterrence has been, all along, a principal driving force behind SDI. What has been so disturbing to them about Reagan's dream, which calls for a total defense against missiles shared by European allies and Soviets alike, is that it implies the end of U.S. or any other nuclear deterrence for Europe.[11] Its technological implausibility for Europe is not what arouses the Europeans' objections. On the contrary, only the general implausibility of SDI reconciles European governments to it. While the goal of a world free from offensive nuclear weapons doubtless appeals to publics in Europe as in the United States, it has no appeal at all to NATO governments, all of which have firmly embraced the strategy of nuclear deterrence. When the issues have been clearly posed, moreover, these governments have been sustained by their publics.[12]

No one should be surprised at European support for the strategic status quo. Since 1945 Europe has enjoyed a peace nearly as long as between 1870 and 1914, and in much less promising political circumstances. Given the division of Germany and the failure of the Russians to consolidate their hold over major East European countries, so enduring a peace would be difficult to imagine under the prenuclear military conditions of 1939.

This is not simply another way of saying that, without nuclear deterrence, the Soviets would have conquered the rest of the continent. A nonnuclear Europe would not necessarily have become a Soviet-dominated Europe. But had there been a European military balance in a nonnuclear world, the Europeans, rather than the Americans, would have had to maintain it. U.S. forces are unlikely to have stayed mobilized for four decades in order to match the Soviets in Eurasia. It is certainly conceivable that, in time, a Western Europe encouraged by the United States could have mobilized its own immense resources to build conventional forces to match the Soviets'. But it is far less conceivable that such forces would have sat immobile for four decades in the absence of any viable political settlement.

Compared to the likely alternatives, the nuclear balance of terror has given West Europeans a very comfortable time. Not only have they been preserved from a war, but the cost to them of their security has been rather low. Since the late 1960s, particularly, they have devoted a substantially smaller proportion of their resources to military costs than in the years before World War I or during the interwar period.[13] The benefits have been manifest for their economic systems and standards of living. Europeans have used their abundance to build political-economic systems that are not without problems, to be sure, but in which the age-old tensions that wracked their societies in the past have been greatly mitigated.

Their security has cost the Europeans so little not only because nuclear deterrence has been much cheaper than conventional forces, but also because the essential nuclear forces for Europe have been provided mainly by the Americans. To this day NATO remains essentially a nuclear protectorate of the United States.

As everyone knows, "extended deterrence" has grown increasingly difficult. Until the 1960s NATO and U.S. strategic predominance went hand in hand. NATO provided the forward bases that gave the United States its ability to strike the Soviets. Even with nuclear weapons, the Soviets, lacking similar bases, could retaliate only on U.S. allies. The development of intercontinental missiles effectively ended U.S. invulnerability and, eventually, U.S. strategic superiority as well. Under the circumstances, the risks for the United States of extended deterrence have, in theory at least, increased dramatically.

Discussions of U.S.-Soviet strategic balance often tend to ignore the critical role of America's extended deterrence for Europe. It is, however, the crux of the nation's strategic problem. Strategists and their computers can dream up innumerable scenarios for confrontation. But given the heroic risks and uncertainties, an unprovoked Soviet nuclear attack on the United States seems a remote possibility. No doubt both sides could work themselves into such a state of collective hysteria that such extremities begin to seem imaginable. But whatever the fantasies and terrors of the target planners, the nuclear balance is extremely robust. Europe aside, no direct conflict between Americans and Soviets could remotely justify running such risks.

In Europe, however, the superpowers do have a point of direct contact over a geopolitical stake so vital to both that an intercontinental nuclear war does become imaginable. Despite forty years of peace, Europe's political conditions still seem fundamentally unstable. The continent's artificial division remains. The Red Army still sits over a restive Eastern Europe. Germany remains split down the middle. In this nuclear era hardly anyone imagines any European state deliberately starting a war to change the status quo. All the same, it is not easy to imagine Europe going on forever in its present state. The basic political instability is attested to by the large military forces that continue to confront each other on both sides. In recent years, despite some apparent progress in reaching a more comfortable pan-European modus vivendi, these forces have not diminished but increased substantially.[14] The United States, meanwhile, remains the principal guarantor of West European security.

The clear and present danger to U.S. security, in short, has been that a war might start over Europe. How to deter such a war, and what to do if it occurs, has been the chief driving concern of U.S. nuclear strategy since the 1950s.

Since strategic superiority began to fade, the United States has never been able to find a satisfactory resolution.[15] While technological reality imposed the doctrine of mutual assured destruction, it was the European commitment that inspired flexible response and, later, counterforce strategy. The essential point of the strategy is that any engagement over Europe should be limited as much as possible to the minimum needed to stop the Soviet thrust. While the logic of flexible response called for a genuine balance of conventional forces, in reality the Europeans have been unwilling and the Americans incapable of providing such forces. Instead, they have compromised on a NATO with just enough conventional forces to prevent an easy Soviet conventional victory on the ground. Any Soviet attack will mean a major battle, with several hundred thousand American soldiers involved. Such a prospect makes a U.S. resort to nuclear weapons probable, and thus makes more plausible the nuclear deterrence upon which NATO's defense really depends.

In effect, Americans have had to content themselves with a very expensive NATO that nevertheless falls short of providing a real conventional balance. A NATO first use of nuclear weapons has therefore never been far in the background. The thrust of American strategic thinking, as opposed to European, has been to limit the scope of nuclear use as tightly as possible. From the 1950s on, NATO has planned on using small-yield nuclear weapons to stop numerically superior advancing Soviet forces. Over the years flexible response has been elaborated into a hierarchy of specific target sets designed to raise the level of nuclear force just sufficiently to stop the Soviet thrust without precipitating an all-out intercontinental war.

Once multiple independently targeted reentry vehicle (MIRV) technology created the possibility of a greatly expanded number of highly accurate warheads, flexible response evolved into counterforce strategy. With such a strategy, even a European war that escalated into an intercontinental exchange could be spun out into a protracted and strictly limited test of will. Precise attacks and counterattacks could be directed at enemy missiles, moreover, rather than at enemy cities.

The U.S. lead in MIRVs provided the technology that made a counterforce strategy plausible. America's consequent and very substantial lead in warheads gave it "escalation dominance," which meant that the United States could, at various limited stages of nuclear escalation, reasonably hope to present the Soviets with a calculus of punishment and gain that made it more rational for them to back down than to escalate.

Counterforce strategy, however, has not been a satisfactory resolution for America's strategic problem of extended deterrence. The technological lead upon which the strategy was based has not proved `stable. The Soviets have gradually acquired MIRV technology of their own. Since they have always concentrated on comparatively large land-based missiles, MIRVing has allowed the Soviets to catch up rapidly, threatening to surpass the Americans in numbers of land-based warheads.[16] This, in turn, has led to American apprehensions about a "window of vulnerability." A Soviet first strike could, in theory, destroy the bulk of U.S. land-based missiles. Thus disarmed, America might decline to retaliate. Hence, the pressure for mobile missiles, ballistic missile defense, and now SDI.[17]

The whole situation has its ironic side. The MIRV technology that was to have permitted a limited first strike by the United States to stop a conventional attack on Western Europe has now led to widespread American fears of a Soviet first strike on the United States. Technology has escaped from its original strategic context and now threatens both sides with a manic arms race undisciplined by any real strategic interest other than countering the most recent innovations of the other. As a practical matter, the United States has now grown more directly and acutely vulnerable than ever before.

All of this would be easier to dismiss as merely a strategist's fantasy were it not for the continuing U.S. protectorate for Western Europe. That commitment, still nuclear-based because Western Europe will not build an adequate conventional deterrent, holds despite the radical deterioration in the United States' own strategic position. The United States' strategic dilemma is that the obligation to Europe requires America to prepare for an early first use of nuclear weapons, but it no longer has sufficient technological dominance to rely comfortably on making such a threat.[18]

From this perspective SDI has a double meaning. In theory, it could be seen as a way to escape from this strategic dilemma over the European protectorate. A United States once more invulnerable to nuclear attack, or whose deterrent is far more effectively protected, would be in a much better position to confirm its extended geopolitical engagements. But the president's rhetoric embodies a purely defensive strategy for SDI. It proposes to abolish offensive nuclear weapons and share the SDI technology with the Soviets. The president's rhetoric seems, in effect, a renunciation of extended deterrence for Europe. Thus, the rhetoric troubles Europeans far more than any actual military program.

European unhappiness with U.S. fashions in deterrence is hardly new. Europeans have always been intellectually uneasy with flexible response and counterforce strategies.[19] Limiting escalation in a European war has always been a predominantly American concern. European strategists have generally argued that deterrence is greater when the threat of all-out war is most immediate. If Europe is to be destroyed, in other words, why not the United States and Russia, too? The certain prospect that a war in Europe would automatically ruin both superpowers seems, in European perspectives, the best defense against such a war ever occurring. For Europeans, plans for a limited nuclear war in Europe conjure up visions of a superpower nuclear tournament, with Eastern and Western Europe the playing field. Early in the postwar era the British and French thought it prudent to develop their own nuclear forces, conceived of as "triggers" to turn an attack on themselves into a nuclear war by attacking the Soviet homeland regardless of what the Americans were doing. European and American strategic views are fundamentally different mainly because the two sides of the Atlantic are in different geopolitical situations when it comes to European deterrence. Europe's own limited nuclear forces exist to retaliate against an attack on themselves, not on their allies. While it is even doubtful, for example, that French nuclear forces would engage themselves in the defense of Germany, unless France also saw itself as being under attack, no one imagines the French force being used if the Soviets attacked the United States but left Europe alone.

All Europeans, of course, are not in the same situation. Of the West European powers, only Britain and France have nuclear weapons of their own. West Germany and Italy, along with the smaller NATO powers, rely entirely on the United States. The

British nuclear deterrent depends on U.S. technology and is integrated in NATO, although it is subject to national control in a supreme emergency.[20] The French deterrent is completely national in origin and control. But its only unambiguous purpose, according to declared French strategy, is to retaliate if France itself is attacked by nuclear forces or is about to be overrun by conventional forces. French strategy has long contemplated using tactical nuclear forces against advancing Soviet forces in Germany, not so much to defend Germany as to demonstrate a willingness to proceed to an all-out nuclear attack against Soviet cities to defend France. An all-out threat obviously seems most plausible, and therefore is most deterring, when a country is defending its own territory and independence. It grows less so, and therefore is less deterring, in defense of an ally. It seems weaker still when meant to cover an ally against a conventional, not a nuclear, attack. In other words, France, with its limited force, can threaten a massive attack on Soviet cities to defend itself, while the United States cannot so plausibly threaten massive retaliation for a Soviet conventional invasion of Germany. Since the Americans could not, and the Europeans would not provide NATO with an adequate conventional deterrent, the U.S. commitment rests upon an early NATO use of nuclear weapons. Under the circumstances, the United States has looked for a way to use these nuclear forces in a selective and limited fashion. This explains the American predilection for flexible response and counterforce strategies, as opposed to French enthusiasm for massive retaliation.[21]

Despite their intellectual disagreements with the Americans, the French have found a very comfortable position within the American protectorate. Given their own diffidence about extending their deterrent, they have never had any trouble understanding American uneasiness. It was precisely because of doubts about whether the United States—or any other country—would sustain the risks of extended deterrence that the French insisted upon pressing ahead with their own nuclear force. Their *force de dissuasion* was designed to ensure that if France were devastated, the Soviet Union itself would not escape devastation regardless of the U.S. reaction. The Soviets in turn would be unlikely to suffer the grievous damage of a French attack without retaliating against their principal nuclear adversary, the United States. Thus, any major European war involving France was likely to be both nuclear and intercontinental. As the French saw it, their force not only reduced the likelihood of a nuclear contest between the superpowers conducted in Europe alone but also enhanced U.S. deterrence for Europe. Thanks to the French "trigger," the Soviets would not start any confrontation in Europe unless they were prepared for mutual suicide.

To some extent the French deterrent can be seen to benefit Western Europe as a whole. While the French have never yet promised a nuclear riposte to an attack on their West German ally, French ground forces remain in Germany and are equipped with nuclear weapons. A second nuclear force among Germany's allies, in itself, increases "uncertainty," and hence, according to French doctrine, it increases deterrence. The French now and then have described their nuclear force as being held "in reserve for Europe." They have, nevertheless, carefully refrained from making precise commitments to their German neighbors, despite extensive bilateral discussion during the past several years. To underscore their complete self-determination of their own obligations and interests, they have kept their forces independent from the NATO command since 1966. They remain within the Atlantic alliance but cooperate only selectively with its integrated military structure.

In effect, the French have their cake and eat it, too. They can avoid any more intimate and committed involvement in the collective continental defense because they can presume a U.S. defense that covers France as well. The French have thus greatly reduced the price and enhanced the quality of their national security. With a proportional defense budget regularly one-half to two-thirds of the American, they have managed to build a respectable strategic force, including nuclear submarines, as well as formidable conventional forces for global interventions.[22] Forces for conventional defense still receive a relatively low priority, not, presumably, because the French are uninterested in the territorial defense of Europe, but because they believe this task can be left mainly to the Germans and Americans. One consequence is to make a genuine conventional balance impossible. With their faith in nuclear deterrence, the French do not believe that one is needed.

Like the Germans, and in strained but durable cooperation with them, the French have mounted a persistent campaign to improve Europe's general political relations with the Soviets.[23] The French have also promoted West European economic and political cooperation, and a special Franco-German relationship in particular, to speed modernization of the French economy and to provide a reasonably effective counterweight to the giant U.S. economy. In short, within the present nuclear and geopolitical dispensation, France has managed to achieve a high degree both of security and prosperity.

Among the major European countries, Germany is geopolitically the least comfortable. The border between its two halves constitutes the front line between Western and Eastern systems. It is among the West Germans that the notion of transatlantic ''coupling'' has received its most elaborate development. Lacking nuclear weapons of their own, German strategic theorists argue that the alliance rests, in effect, on the European perception that the United States and Western Europe share an equivalent vulnerability.[24] Thanks to that perception, Germans can tolerate U.S. missiles based on their soil and can control their twin fears: that the United States will not defend them or that it will involve them in a limited war having little to do with Germany's own interests. SDI, German analysts insist, inevitably emphasizes the unequal vulnerability of Europe and its U.S. protector, thus threatening the psychological constitution of the Atlantic alliance. Needless to say, this view of the alliance has never had wide currency in the United States. If it did, the United States would probably leave NATO.

In a more realistic vein, the Germans have taken serious steps to assuage American worries about the growing vulnerabilities of extended deterrence. One palliative is stronger NATO conventional forces to give greater credibility to flexible response. The Germans have long provided the backbone of NATO's conventional forces, and thanks to them, the United States is not likely to be called upon to use nuclear weapons to stop a limited thrust across the frontier.[25]

At the same time, the West Germans have improved the European diplomatic and political atmosphere. Mostly on their own initiative, they took advantage of the superpower détente of the late 1960s and 1970s to reach a broad political modus vivendi with the Soviets, the East Germans, and the rest of Eastern Europe. They recognized the status quo, including the existence of a separate East German state, and renounced the use of force to change that status quo. In their own complicated formula they accepted the notion of ''two states in one German nation.'' While they have not renounced hopes that "peaceful change" may bring some eventual national reunification, the prevalent formula for that reunification is not the old Bismarckian Reich, which was a centralized imperial state. Instead it is something closer to the confederal models that predated the Bismarckian creation. In effect, as is commonly said, German unification can take place only in the context of peaceful European unification—a long-range vision designed to keep alive hope for the future without arousing fears in the present.[26]

German diplomatic concepts have been successful not only in improving and stabilizing relations with the East but also in enlisting the support of the West European allies—most notably France, which had its own vision of a "Europe from the Atlantic to the Urals." Thanks to robust West European support for this German-crafted pan-European détente, the deteriorating superpower relations of the 1980s have not brought about a comparable degeneration of East-West relations within Europe itself. One reason is undoubtedly the shared stake—on both sides—in East-West trade. German money has greatly aided German diplomacy. Despite Eastern Europe's severe economic problems in the depressed 1980s, the long-term political-economic prospects have seemed sufficiently promising for Western Europe to resist stoutly the strong American pressures to limit economic relations. West European governments will be on their guard that SDI not become a powerful U.S. lever to control their Eastern trade.[27]

Given their painful historical situation, the Germans have made themselves comfortable within the present strategic arrangement. In the face of unpromising geopolitical circumstances, the U.S. deterrent has given them more military security than they have enjoyed since well before World War I, and at an economic cost greatly inferior to their military burdens of the past. In addition, they have parlayed their military dependence into a promising diplomatic accommodation with the East that increases their present security without decreasing their future prospects.

Not surprisingly, neither the French nor the German political elites, nor those of any other NATO country, wish to see radical changes in the current transatlantic security relationship or strategy. Extended deterrence under the American protectorate has suited them well enough. Other West Europeans are like the Germans. They have never known invulnerability at any period of their history, and they do not expect it now. They rate the actual risks to their security exceptionally low by comparison with nearly any other modern period. This high security, moreover, comes exceptionally cheap. They are nearly all spending a relatively low proportion of their national incomes on defense, compared to present U.S. or their own historical standards. Considering the Europeans' dependence on it, U.S. military protection does not unbearably constrain their economic or diplomatic independence. In the French case it hardly limits their military independence.

Pressure for change is naturally much stronger on the American side. For a country accustomed to invulnerability, the risks of extended deterrence have grown increasingly hard to bear. Weak NATO conventional forces mean that the United States must be prepared for a first use of nuclear weapons to fulfill its NATO commitment. Only possession of clear strategic superiority, if not outright invulnerability, can make the United States truly comfortable with such a commitment.

It may be argued that the United States must and can learn to live with this burden. Considering the stake, the United States cannot disengage from European defense, and the existing NATO arrangement is less uncomfortable than any conceivable alternative. This view might have been held more complacently before the Reagan administration and SDI. It seems less easy to hold it now. Even if the Reagan administration's strategic views seem highly idiosyncratic, they have behind them a decade of mounting U.S. dissatisfaction with the country's strategic posture. The widespread clamor against the "window of vulnerability," the disillusionment with arms control, and the pressures for "no first use," upgrading conventional forces, and European burden-sharing all suggest the growing instability of any American strategic consensus, including, implicitly, the commitment to extended deterrence for Europe.

In effect, counterforce strategy—designed to preserve the plausibility of American first use for Europe—requires U.S. superiority. Once the Soviets acquired MIRV technology, and hence parity, it became impossible to stabilize the nuclear balance in a fashion adequate for U.S. purposes. No arms agreement was satisfactory because no arms negotiator could reasonably expect the Soviets to concede to Americans the superiority needed to keep extended deterrence safe for the United States.

Is SDI a solution for extended deterrence? In theory it might be. If the United States were invulnerable to the Soviets while the Soviets remained vulnerable to U.S. nuclear forces, a U.S. nuclear commitment to Western Europe could be sustained with impunity. If SDI also made Western Europe invulnerable to nuclear attack while leaving the Soviets vulnerable, NATO's problems with extended deterrence would presumably be over. If the United States were invulnerable but Western Europe and the Soviets were not, then the old problems of the 1950s and 1960s would reappear. Those Europeans without effective nuclear deterrents of their own would feel that they were Soviet hostages for American good behavior. An invulnerable United States might grow too bellicose, and Europe would feel Soviet retaliation. But these fears were manageable before and doubtless could be managed again.

None of this speculation is very realistic because it is all based on technological fantasy. Few analysts expect SDI to give the United States anything approaching invulnerability. At best, SDI may give U.S. land-based ICBMs better protection, which is still unlikely to provide a stable margin of superiority. And since Western Europe is open to so many kinds of nuclear attack, not to mention an overwhelming conventional invasion, expectations are still lower for what SDI can offer European security. By taking funds away from conventional defense or by increasing the cost of Europe's own nuclear deterrents, SDI's net military effects are likely to be harmful. Politically, by raising all the thorny issues of extended deterrence and decoupling, without offering any real chance of improvement, the net effect is also harmful.

Similarly, insofar as SDI blocks progress on arms control and further deteriorates superpower relations, or appears to do so, it may undermine the political modus vivendi in Europe itself. Most Europeans see pan-European political understandings as a major component for their security. Insofar as SDI seems to defeat the apparent efforts of the Gorbachev regime to cool the arms race and proceed with modernization of the Soviet economy, Europeans are likely to blame the United States for missing a historic opportunity for a radical improvement of pan-European security.[28] In short, SDI is unlikely to resolve the dilemmas of extended deterrence. Instead, it will make them worse.

Quite apart from the intellectual instability of American deterrence theory, another powerful solvent is now dissolving the strategic status quo: America's structural and fiscal deficit and its heavy, rapidly growing foreign indebtedness. The fiscal imbalance and consequent monetary gyrations and external imbalances have seriously disturbed both domestic and world economies. In due course, powerful pressures arising from the fiscal situation seem bound to force a reconsideration of military priorities. Enthusiasm for a new and expensive strategic program like SDI would only intensify the squeeze. The very high cost of maintaining standing conventional forces for Western Europe obviously makes existing NATO arrangements a ripe target. Moreover, U.S. pressure for European burden-sharing has been swelling for over a decade.

That the transatlantic military relationship has grown unjustifiably lopsided has long been widely admitted. The American nuclear protectorate over Europe, undertaken in the conditions of the late 1940s and early 1950s, clearly stands in need of revision in the very different strategic and economic conditions of the 1980s. If all SDI did was to precipitate that revision, it would be no bad thing.[29] Unfortunately, it also threatens to deteriorate superpower relations, highlight insoluble strategic questions within the alliance, and undermine further the alliance's conventional forces. On the face of it, none of this sets a propitious climate for successful revisions in the alliance.

Obviously, so long as the future shape of SDI remains so indefinable, predicting its consequences for the alliance is conjectural. In the worst case the United States, having spent a great deal of money for a marginal improvement in the survivability of its land-based missiles, would diminish its conventional commitment to Europe without any corresponding economic benefit. As the Soviets deployed their own defensive systems, European nuclear deterrents would seem devalued. For France and Britain, demands for increased spending on conventional forces would be paralleled by demands for strategic upgrading. Europeans, feeling beleaguered, would blame the Americans for spoiling the opportunity for a more solid détente in order to ratchet up the arms race. Not even the usual ham-fisted Soviet diplomacy would quell a powerful European impulse toward accommodation with the Soviets—and from a position of military weakness and alienation from the United States. Such conditions are unlikely, moreover, to encourage much solidarity among the West Europeans themselves.

A best case can be imagined from the obverse of the worst. The strategic and budgetary effects of SDI might finally precipitate the fundamental and long-needed reorganization of the alliance. Europeans at last would be provoked into creating a more balanced and autonomous defense. To sustain it, France, Germany, and perhaps even Britain would reach a more serious political and military consensus among themselves. Such an evolution would not break the American link or end extended deterrence. Europeans would assume primary responsibility for organizing conventional defense, but some U.S. forces would continue to be involved. A stronger European nuclear force would be created, but the U.S. commitment would remain. The emphasis would merely shift from extended to multiple deterrence.

Logically, a more indigenous defense should not lessen European security, particularly if fiscal pressures reduce the U.S. contribution in any event. A more Europeanized NATO could greatly improve the general psychological mood of transatlantic relations. American resentments and pretensions should decline with American hegemony, and a less dependent Europe should also grow less pusillanimous. The primordial common interest in containing Soviet power in Eurasia should be less encumbered on both sides.

At the same time, a militarily more self-sufficient Europe should also be in a better position to pursue containment through cooperative diplomacy with the East. A long-term strategy of trying to domesticate the Soviet regime within a pan-European system is certainly not bad in itself provided it is based on West European strength and unity rather than despairing weakness and disunity. Further insulating détente in Europe from the vagaries of U.S.-Soviet relations should actually strengthen the Atlantic alliance.

A new equilibrium within NATO should also help superpower relations. With the United States relieved of its too exclusive responsibility for European defense, the pressure for the arms race ought logically to diminish. In short, in the best case SDI will provoke devolution, and it is only devolution, rather than SDI, that can relieve the problems of extended deterrence.

Successful devolution within NATO, however, may seem even more fantastic than President Reagan's dreams for SDI. A common view sees Europe incapable of rising to such an occasion. The alleged

feebleness of the European states, however, has been greatly exaggerated, as well as manipulated, to dampen any initiative for
change. Europeans have all along behaved logically, given the U.S.
commitment, with no sign of diminished concern for self-interest
or self-preservation. Since SDI cannot resolve the problems of extended deterrence, but may well leave the United States still less
able to sustain the present arrangements, devolution seems NATO's
only real option, short of an end to the Atlantic alliance altogether.

Such conclusions about Europe suggest a different direction
for U.S. strategic thought and policy than is customary among either
advocates or opponents of SDI. It is true that the old faith in deterrence and arms control has shown considerable powers of
resistance. Those faithful to the traditional doctrines form a large
part of the U.S. political establishment and are in a broad conspiracy
to withstand the SDI frenzy. Considering SDI in relation to Europe,
however, suggests that preserving deterrence requires a bolder
strategy than simply clinging to the traditional formulas. The strategic instability that drives the arms race and inspires SDI stems,
in good part, from the U.S. nuclear commitment to Europe. It is
the tension inherent in extended deterrence that has goaded
counterforce strategy to its present manic extreme. Relief cannot
come merely from well-intentioned efforts to promote U.S.-Soviet
self-restraint and agreement. Something must also reduce the too
heavy burden that extended deterrence lays on U.S. nuclear strategy. So long as Europe's defense rests so exclusively on a U.S. first
use of nuclear weapons, nothing short of superiority will ever
soothe American anxieties and nothing short of Soviet capitula-
tion will end the arms race.

Devolution of European defense is not, of course, a panacea.
For a start, it can only be partial. Realistically, the United States
probably cannot, and certainly should not, escape engagement in
European defense. But the American strategic burden would be
far more manageable if the Europeans took over the primary responsibility for running their own defense and NATO evolved from a
nuclear protectorate into a nuclear alliance. Such an evolution would
bring U.S. commitments into some reasonable relation with U.S.
resources. Today's stubbornly bipolar strategic culture would begin
to come to terms with the world's pluralistic economic and political
system.

How is it that so much of U.S. strategic thought ignores the real problems of American security? Why has a vision as improbable and disruptive as the original SDI been taken so seriously? All branches of specialized learning have a tendency to become a sort of cult, cut off from any broader historical, political, or philosophical foundation that might keep them anchored to the real world. Postwar economics, for example, has increasingly become a sort of faddish technology for producing miracles.[30] And industrial technology has too often embraced technical improvements in efficiency that carry much heavier long-term environmental or social costs.

Part of the explanation for this narrowness is doubtless sociological. Specialization seems natural to mass-produced, upwardly mobile elites who, as "experts," can feel confident without the need for any broader and more comprehensive education, even in their own specialties. Thus, for example, economists can become technicians, reared narrowly in one sect or another, with little knowledge of economic history or the development of economic theory. The same process has characterized nuclear strategy, which has gradually isolated itself not only from politics and economics but from any comprehensive view of military strategy itself. When a society as a whole loses its capacity to resist these cults, when, in other words, it loses its common sense, then the nation is headed for trouble. The administration's freakish enthusiasm for SDI as a technological remedy for all our geopolitical problems, not to mention the lemming-like conversion of much of the strategic and technological elites, seems a symptom of a certain cultural decadence afflicting our society. It is an unhappy reversal of stereotypes that the Europeans seem so much more robust in their common sense. It would be a happy irony to have Europe bring us back to our senses.

NOTES

1. See the March 23, 1983 "Address to the Nation by President Ronald Reagan: Peace and National Security," *Department of State Bulletin* 83, no. 2073 (Washington, D.C.: GPO, 1983), 8–14. See also Reagan arms-control adviser Paul Nitze's caution that BMD systems should not be deployed unless "cost-effective at the margin...that is, they must be cheap enough to add additional defensive capability

so that the other side has no incentive to add additional offensive capacity to overcome the defense." *The New York Times,* February 21, 1985. The president himself, after the October 1986 U.S.-Soviet summit in Iceland, described the strategic defense effort merely as "insurance" against Soviet cheating on arms agreements. *The New York Times,* October 14, 1986.

For the ambivalent conclusions of the president's own expert panels, see "Strategic Defense and Anti-Satellite Weapons," hearings before the Committee on Foreign Relations, U.S. Senate, 98th Cong., 2d sess., April 25, 1984, 94–175; Donald L. Hafner, "Assessing the President's Vision: The Fletcher, Miller, and Hoffman Panels," in *Weapons in Space,* vol. 1 ("Concepts and Technologies"), *Daedalus* 114, no. 2 (Spring 1985), 91–107; and John C. Toomay, a member of the Fletcher panel, "The Case for Ballistic Missile Defense," in *Weapons in Space,* vol. 2 ("Implications for Security"), *Daedalus* 114, no. 3 (Summer 1985), 219–37. For the uneasy intellectual coexistence between Reagan's original exalted vision and the more prosaic rationales offered by most SDI proponents, see former secretary of defense James R. Schlesinger, "Rhetoric and Reality in Star Wars," *International Security* 10, no. 1 (Summer 1985), 6, or George Rathjens and Jack Ruina, "BMD and Strategic Instability," *Weapons in Space,* vol. 2, 255.

2. For a sampling of arguments against the continental bubble, see Schlesinger, "Rhetoric and Reality in Star Wars"; Rathjens and Ruina, "BMD and Strategic Instability"; or Hans A. Bethe, Jeffrey Boutwell, and Richard L. Garwin, "BMD Technologies and Concepts in the 1980s," in *Weapons in Space,* vol. 1, 53–72. For the vulnerability of satellites, see Ashton B. Carter, "The Relationship of ASAT and BMD Systems," in *Weapons in Space,* vol. 1, 171–89; Kurt Gottfried and Richard Ned Lebow, "Anti-Satellite Weapons: Weighing the Risks," in *Weapons in Space,* vol. 1, 147–70; and Harold Brown, "Is SDI Technically Feasible?" *Foreign Affairs* ("America and the World 1985"), 64, no. 3, 442–47.

3. Europe, much closer to the Soviets, is far more vulnerable to cruise missiles, bombers, nuclear artillery, and so on. Shorter-range missiles, moreover, have a much shallower trajectory that makes them correspondingly more difficult to intercept. Paul Gallis, Mark Lowenthal, and Marcia Smith, *The Strategic Defense Initiative and United States Alliance Strategy* (Washington, D.C.: Congressional Research Service Report No. 85–48F, 1985).

4. A distinction must be made between costs at the margin for offensive and defensive systems already built and overall costs of developing and deploying the systems in the first place. Opponents of the bubble argue that even marginal exchange costs favor offense, whereas many admit that the reckoning of marginal exchange costs for point defense is less clear-cut. For example, "preferential" point defense—secretly choosing a fraction of offensive missile silos to defend— might obtain improved marginal exchange costs. This is because the enemy, not knowing which silos are defended, would be forced to throw additional warheads against all of them to have any reasonable chance of preventing a retaliatory second strike. The overall costs of the bubble are, of course, enormous, although the value of what is being defended, for example, the entire U.S. population, is priceless. Point defense, with far less overall cost, also covers targets, for example, missiles or bases, whose own value is far less. Its cost, therefore, must be weighed against the cost of ensuring a second-strike ability by other means—for instance, deploying additional offensive missiles. For definitions, estimates, and arguments, see

Barry M. Blechman and Victor A. Utgoff, *Fiscal and Economic Implications of Strategic Defenses* (Boulder, Colo.: Copublished by Westview Press and The Johns Hopkins Foreign Policy Institute, 1986), 25; Rathjens and Ruina, "BMD and Strategic Instability," 242–50; Brown, "Is SDI Technically Feasible?" 444–45; Toomay, "The Case for Ballistic Missile Defense," 224–25; and Schlesinger, "Rhetoric and Reality in Star Wars," 7.

5. John C. Toomay, supposedly advocating BMD, in fact renders a most damning indictment along these lines. ("The Case for Ballistic Missile Defense," 232.) See also the chapter by Robert W. Tucker in this book; Schlesinger, "Rhetoric and Reality in Star Wars," 10; and Jerry Hough, "Soviet Interpretation and Response," in *Arms Control and the Strategic Defense Initiative: Three Perspectives* (Muscatine, Iowa: The Stanley Foundation, Occasional Paper 36, 1985). Rathjens and Ruina, because they deprecate the feasibility of the bubble, are not worried about instability in a crisis but rather about the tremendous new impetus to the U.S.-Soviet arms race. See "BMD and Strategic Instability."

6. See Thierry de Montbrial, "The European Dimension," *Foreign Affairs* ("America and the World 1985"), 64, no. 3, and Samuel F. Wells, Jr., "The United States and European Defense Cooperation," *Survival* 27, no. 4 (July/August 1985), 162–65.

7. Both Britain and France prefer today's barring of nationwide BMD systems by the ABM treaty but do not depend on it for the viability of their deterrence. See the interview with then French defense minister M. Paul Quilès, "La défense spatiale ne rend pas caduque l'arme nucléaire," *Le Monde*, December 18, 1985; and Benoît d'Aboville (French Ministry for Foreign Affairs) and M. Guionnet (French National Space Agency), "How BMD and ASAT New Developments Could Affect Third Countries," unpublished paper (Paris: June 1985), 16. See also Lawrence Freedman, "The Small Nuclear Powers," in Ashton B. Carter and David N. Schwartz, eds., *Ballistic Missile Defense* (Washington, D.C.: The Brookings Institution, 1984). For the current and planned configurations of British nuclear forces, see Secretary of State for Defence (U.K.), *Statement on the Defence Estimates 1985*, no. 1 (London: Her Majesty's Stationery Office, 1985), 19–21, 54. For France, see David S. Yost, "France's Deterrent Posture and Security in Europe, Part 1: Capabilities and Doctrine," *Adelphi Papers*, no. 194 (London: International Institute for Strategic Studies, Winter 1984/85), 19–29.

8. See *Strengthening Conventional Deterrence in Europe, Proposals for the 1980s*, Report of the European Security Study (Boston, Mass.: American Academy of Arts and Sciences, 1983), 7–36, 153–54.

9. Most analysts decline to estimate the potential cost in any specific manner. The oft-cited figure of $1 trillion seems intended to convey only an order of magnitude. A major exception is found in Blechman and Utgoff, *Fiscal and Economic Implications of Strategic Defenses*. For various versions of strategic defense, their figures range from $160 billion to $770 billion. But the authors concede that their estimates are based on some optimistic assumptions that become more questionable as the systems projected become more advanced. For instance, while some Soviet countermeasures are projected, increasing the number of Russian ICBMs is not. The authors themselves appear to rebut their own most important

assumption: "that the Soviet Union's antisatellite effort could be countered effectively for costs on the order of those described for the satellites used in the systems. *There is little basis for this assumption.* The potential vulnerability of defense satellites to attacks appears to be perhaps the largest unsolved problem for strategic defenses, and we are unaware of any promising solutions to it" (101, emphasis added).

10. It is not possible to make a precise calculation of the share of the U.S. military budget that is devoted to defending Europe. Brief reflection, however, can suggest the magnitude. Roughly 40 percent of the defense budget is manpower cost. Roughly one-third of the army's standing divisions are in Europe; another third have European defense as their primary mission. These "heavy" divisions have enormous associated capital expenditures, including major equipment and ammunition. In addition to the army divisions stationed in the United States but with Europe as their primary mission, the United States is obligated to supply eighty-eight air force squadrons and one marine amphibious brigade as reinforcements within ten days of the outbreak of hostilities. See *The Military Balance: 1985–86* (London: International Institute for Strategic Studies, 1985), 13; U.S. Department of Defense, *Report on Allied Contributions to the Common Defense* (citation), 76, 81; and Caspar Weinberger, *Annual Report to the Congress, Fiscal Year 1986* (Washington, D.C.: Department of Defense, 1985), 224.

Earl Ravenal has estimated the annual cost of the U.S. force commitment to Europe, for general purpose forces, to be $134 billion. ("Europe Without America: The Erosion of NATO," *Foreign Affairs* 63, no. 5 [Summer 1985].) For an extended but older version of this argument, see Earl C. Ravenal, *Defining Defense: The 1985 Military Budget* (Washington, D.C.: CATO Institute, 1984). Reduction of the U.S. commitment to European ground defense might also imply considerable reductions in the Reagan plans for a 600-ship navy. For the official justification of a 600-ship navy, see the statement of John F. Lehman, Jr., secretary of the navy, hearings before the Committee on Armed Services, U.S. Senate, 97th Cong., 2d sess. (Washington, D.C.: GPO, 1982), part 2, 1054–72. For a critique, see Joshua M. Epstein, *The 1987 Defense Budget* (Washington, D.C.: The Brookings Institution, 1986), 41–45.

11. See Christoph Bertram, "Strategic Defense and the Western Alliance," in *Weapons in Space*, vol. 2, 276–96.

12. For the views and prospects of various peace movements, see Werner Kaltefleiter and Robert L. Pfaltzgraff, eds., *The Peace Movements in Europe and the United States* (New York: St. Martin's Press, 1983). For recent polls of European opinion, see *SIPRI Yearbook 1986* (Oxford: Oxford University Press, 1986), 28–32. For an analysis of the West German elections of 1983, in which missile deployment was a key issue, see Arthur M. Hanhardt, "International Politics and the 1983 Election," in H. G. Peter Wallach and George K. Romoser, eds., *West German Politics in the Mid-Eighties, Crisis and Continuity* (New York: Praeger, 1985), 219–34.

13.

DEFENSE EXPENDITURE AS A PERCENTAGE OF GNP

	1914[a]	1938[b]	1949	1954	1965	1969	1974	1977	1980[c]	1983[c]
USA	—	1.5	5.1	12.7	8.3	9.6	6.6	6.0	5.6	7.4
FRG	4.6	—	—	4.7	5.0	4.1	4.1	3.4	3.3	3.4
France	4.8	6.6	6.2	8.5	6.1	4.9	4.1	3.6	4.0	4.2
U.K.	3.4	5.8	7.0	9.9	6.6	5.8	5.8	5.0	5.0	5.5
Italy	3.5	—	3.9	4.5	3.7	3.0	3.0	2.4	2.4	2.8

Source: Except where otherwise noted, data is from Kenneth A. Myers, ed., *NATO: The Next Thirty Years* (Boulder, Colo.: Westview Press, 1980), 406.

[a]A.J.P. Taylor, *The Struggle for Mastery in Europe* (Oxford: Oxford University Press, 1954), xxix.
[b]Study for the Joint Committee on the Economic Report, *Trends in Economic Growth* (Washington, D.C.: GPO, 1955), 276.
[c]*The Military Balance: 1985–86* (London: International Institute for Strategic Studies, 1985), 170.

14.

NATO AND WARSAW PACT FORCES IN EUROPE

	1976		1985	
	NATO	Warsaw Pact	NATO	Warsaw Pact
Combat and Direct Support Troops[a]	1,175,000	1,305,000	2,088,000	2,685,000
Tanks	11,000	26,500	20,333	52,600
Tactical Aircraft	2,960	5,300	4,056	6,159[b]
IRBMs	18[c]	—	18[c]	381
MRBMs	—	—	54	—
GLCMs	—	—	64	—
SRBMs	262	300	261	1,396

Source: Data from *The Military Balance: 1976–77* (London: International Institute for Strategic Studies, 1980), 76, 99, 101, 102; and *The Military Balance: 1985–86*, 186–87, 165–66.

[a]Recent inclusion of previously excluded support troops in the calculation of troop strength makes year-to-year comparisons difficult. However, the figures for missiles, aircraft, and tanks demonstrate the buildup.
[b]Estimated.
[c]French IRBMs.

15. For a general history of U.S. strategic problems and doctrines, see Lawrence Freedman, *The Evolution of Nuclear Strategy* (New York: St. Martin's Press, 1981).

16. Ibid., 345–47.

17. Fears of a U.S. "window of vulnerability" were popularized by the "Committee on the Present Danger," a group formed in the late 1970s by conservative critics of U.S. nuclear policy in general and the SALT II treaty in particular. See Charles Tyroller II, ed., *Alerting America, The Papers of the Committee on The Present Danger* (Washington, D.C.: Pergamon-Brassey's International Defense Publishers, 1984). The thesis was perhaps most notably challenged by President Reagan's own Commission on Strategic Forces, chaired by General Brent Scowcroft. See *Report of the President's Commission on Strategic Forces* (Washington, D.C.: President's Commission on Strategic Forces, April 1983), 7–8, 16–18. For a general account, see Freedman, *The Evolution of Nuclear Strategy*, 372–95. For a similar argument on the link between extended deterrence and the pressure for SDI, see the chapter by Robert W. Tucker in this book; on the link between extended deterrence and counterforce doctrine, see Steven Canby, "The Nuclear Weapons Debate: Is the Framework Right?" chapter in a forthcoming book.

18. Then defense secretary Robert McNamara provided an early and succinct statement of this dilemma when he unveiled "flexible response" as its solution. See "Ann Arbor Speech," June 16, 1962, Department of Defense News Release no. 980.

19. See Michael M. Harrison, *The Reluctant Ally: France and Atlantic Security* (Baltimore, Md.: The Johns Hopkins University Press, 1981), 72–76, 128, and Freedman, *The Evolution of Nuclear Strategy*, 313–29.

20. Lawrence Freedman, "Britain: The First Ex-Nuclear Power?" in *International Security* 6, no. 2 (Fall 1981), 80–104. See also Lawrence Freedman, *Britain and Nuclear Weapons* (London: Macmillan, 1980).

21. For arguments that NATO's conventional forces could or should be improved sufficiently to render a NATO first use or U.S. strategic superiority unnecessary, see Steven Canby and Ingemar Dorfer, "More Troops, Fewer Missiles," *Foreign Policy*, no. 53 (Winter 1983–84), 3–17, or McGeorge Bundy, George F. Kennan, Robert S. McNamara, Gerard Smith, Morton J. Halperin, William W. Kaufmann, Madalene O'Donnell, Leon V. Sigal, Richard H. Ullman, and Paul C. Warnke, "Back From the Brink," *The Atlantic* 258, no. 2 (August 1986), 35–41.

22. For an admirable summary of French doctrines and policies, see Harrison, *The Reluctant Ally*, 134–69. For a concise review of strategy under François Mitterrand, see Robert S. Rudney, "Mitterrand's Defense Concepts: Some Unsocialist Remarks," *Strategic Review* vol. 11, no. 2 (Spring 1983), 20–35; Michael M. Harrison and Simon Serfaty, "A Socialist France and Western Security" (Washington, D.C.: The Johns Hopkins Foreign Policy Institute, 1981), 27–35; or Yost, "France's Deterrent Posture and Security in Europe, Part 1," and "France's Deterrent Posture and Security in Europe, Part 2: Strategic and Arms Control Implications," *Adelphi Papers* no. 195 (London: International Institute for Strategic Studies, Winter 1984/85).

23. For my own analysis of de Gaulle's *Ostpolitik*, see *The Atlantic Fantasy: The U.S., NATO and Europe* (Baltimore, Md.: The Johns Hopkins University Press, 1970). For an update, see my forthcoming study for the Twentieth Century Fund, *America and the Defense of Europe*, chap. 10 and 11.

24. For an example of this view, see Bertram, "Strategic Defense and the Western Alliance."

25.

NATO FORCES IN WEST GERMANY

Belgium	1 corps HQ, 2/3 mechanized division
Canada	1 mechanized brigade
Denmark	None
France	1 corps HQ, 3 armored divisions[a]
Great Britain	1 corps HQ, 4 armored divisions, 1 infantry brigade
The Netherlands	1/3 mechanized division
U.S.	2 corps HQ, 2 armored cavalry regiments, 2 armored divisions, 2 mechanized divisions, 1 armored brigade, 2 mechanized brigades[b]
West Germany	3 corps HQ, 6 armored divisions, 5 mechanized divisions, 3 airborne brigades[c]

Source: Data from William P. Mako, *U.S. Ground Forces and the Defense of Central Europe* (Washington, D.C.: The Brookings Institution, 1983), 50–51.

[a]Excludes a brigade in West Berlin.
[b]Excludes an infantry brigade in West Berlin.
[c]Includes 1 mountain division counted as a mechanized division.

In the mid-1980s, the Bundeswehr has actually been expanding its wartime mobilization level. After 1987, when the Wartime Host Nation Support Programme is fully implemented, wartime strength is to rise to 1.34 million men. Federal Minister of Defense, *The Situation and the Development of the Federal Armed Forces, White Paper 1985* (Bonn: Federal Ministry of Defense, 1985), 236.

26. For Konrad Adenauer's insistence on a Western alliance over a neutralist reunification, see his early collection of speeches, *World Indivisible* (New York: Harper & Brothers, 1955), 49–104. As vice chancellor and foreign minister, Willy Brandt laid out his views on *Ostpolitik*, reunification, and ties to the West in *A Peace Policy for Europe* (New York: Holt, Rinehart and Winston, 1969), especially 94–155. For examples of Chancellor Helmut Kohl's speeches before the Bundestag on the subject of reunification, see "State of the Nation in Divided Germany," *Statements and Speeches* 8, no. 4 (March 5, 1985), and 9, no. 5 (March 18, 1986).

27.
TRADE WITH WARSAW PACT COUNTRIES
(as a percentage of total trade)

	1984		1985	
	Imports	Exports	Imports	Exports
France	3.68	3.17	3.48	2.99
FRG[a]	5.34	4.15	5.09	4.00
Italy	7.20	3.37	5.44	3.33
U.K.	2.23	1.85	1.86	1.51
U.S.	.66	1.92	.56	1.50

Note: Warsaw Pact = Bulgaria, Czechoslovakia, German Democratic Republic, Hungary, Poland, Rumania, and the Soviet Union.

Source: Data from *Monthly Statistics of Foreign Trade* (Washington, D.C.: Organization for Economic Cooperation and Development, August 1986), 50–51, 64–67, 74–75, 90–91.

[a]Excludes trade with the German Democratic Republic.

WEST GERMAN TRADE WITH THE GDR
(as percentage of combined trade with GDR and world)

	1984		1985	
	Imports	Exports	Imports	Exports
FRG	1.75	1.30	1.62	1.45

Source: Calculated from *Country Profile: West Germany 1986–87* (London: The Economist Intelligence Unit, 1986), 31–32.

28. For Soviet economic reform as a principal imperative behind current Soviet arms diplomacy, see Bruce Parrott, *The Soviet Union and Ballistic Missile Defense* (Boulder, Colo.: Copublished by Westview Press and The Johns Hopkins Foreign Policy Institute, 1987). For U.S. SDI as a needed threat to spur advances in Soviet technological capabilities, see Hough, "Soviet Interpretation and Response."

29. For my extended case for devolution of NATO burdens, see *America and the Defense of Europe.*

30. For the gimcrackery of U.S. economic policy, see the conclusion of my *The Imperious Economy* (Cambridge, Mass.: Harvard University Press, 1982).

Other Publications of
The Johns Hopkins University
Foreign Policy Institute

FPI CASE STUDIES

1. *The Panama Canal Negotiations*, Wm. Mark Habeeb and I. William Zartman (1986), $3.50
2. *The New GATT Trade Round*, Charles Pearson and Nils Johnson (1986), $3.50

FPI POLICY STUDY GROUPS

Trade Policy: Three Issues, Isaiah Frank, ed. (1986), $5.00
U.S.-Soviet Relations, Simon Serfaty, ed. (1985), $5.00

FPI POLICY BRIEFS

Arms Control: A Skeptical Appraisal and a Modest Proposal, Robert E. Osgood, April 1986, $3.95
Thinking About SDI, Stephen J. Hadley, March 1986, $3.95
The French Fifth Republic: Steadfast and Changing, Simon Serfaty, February 1986, $3.95
Mexico in Crisis: The Parameters of Accommodation, Bruce Michael Bagley, January 1986, $3.95
The Middle East: Timing and Process, I. William Zartman, January 1986, $3.95
Summit Diplomacy in East-West Relations, Charles H. Fairbanks, Jr., October 1985, $3.95
The Gandhi Visit: Expectations and Realities of the U.S.-Indian Relationship, Thomas Perry Thornton, May 1985 (out of print)
Lebanon: Whose Failure? Barry Rubin, May 1985 (out of print)
Living with the Summits: From Rambouillet to Bonn, Simon Serfaty and Michael M. Harrison, April 1985 (out of print)

SAIS OCCASIONAL PAPERS

America: Images of Empire, Michael Vlahos (1982), $4.75
Tilting at Windmills: Reagan in Central America, Piero Gleijeses, Caribbean Basin Studies Program (1982) (out of print)
American and European Approaches to East-West Relations, Robert E. Osgood (1982), $3.95
A Socialist France and Western Security, Michael M. Harrison and Simon Serfaty (1981), $4.75

SAIS REVIEW

Biannual journal of international affairs, $7.00 (subscription prices vary)

To order copies of these publications contact the FPI Publications Program, School of Advanced International Studies, The Johns Hopkins University, 1740 Massachusetts Avenue, N.W., Washington, D.C. 20036 (202-332-1977)/*SAIS Review* (202-332-1975).

WESTVIEW PRESS/FOREIGN POLICY INSTITUTE

SAIS PAPERS IN INTERNATIONAL AFFAIRS

1. *A Japanese Journalist Looks at U.S.-Japan Relations*, Yukio Matsuyama (1984), $14.00
2. *Report on Cuba: Findings of the Study Group on United States–Cuban Relations*, Central American and Caribbean Program, ed. (1984), $8.50
3. *Peacekeeping on Arab-Israeli Fronts: Lessons from the Sinai and Lebanon*, Nathan A. Pelcovits (1984), $24.00
4. *The Evolution of American Strategic Doctrine: Paul H. Nitze and the Soviet Challenge*, Steven L. Rearden (1984), $19.50
5. *Nuclear Arms Control Choices*, Harold Brown and Lynn E. Davis (1984), $10.50
6. *International Mediation in Theory and Practice*, Saadia Touval and I. William Zartman (1985), $31.00
7. *Report on Guatemala: Findings of the Study Group on United States–Guatemalan Relations*, Central American and Caribbean Program, ed. (1985), $12.00
8. *Contadora and the Central American Peace Process: Selected Documents*, Bruce Michael Bagley, Roberto Alvarez, and Katherine J. Hagedorn, eds. (1985), $32.00
9. *The Making of Foreign Policy in China: Structure and Process*, A. Doak Barnett (1985), $22.00 (hardcover)/$10.95 (softcover)
10. *The Challenge to U.S. Policy in the Third World: Global Responsibilities and Regional Devolution*, Thomas Perry Thornton (1986), $30.00
11. *Defending the Fringe: NATO, the Mediterranean, and the Persian Gulf*, Jed C. Snyder (forthcoming)
12. *Fiscal and Economic Implications of Strategic Defenses*, Barry M. Blechman and Victor A. Utgoff (1986), $22.75
13. *Strategic Defense and the American Ethos: Can the Nuclear World Be Changed?* Michael Vlahos (1986), $15.00
14. *The Soviet Union and Ballistic Missile Defense*, Bruce Parrott (1987)
15. *SDI and U.S. Foreign Policy*, Robert W. Tucker et al. (1987)

To order copies contact Westview Press, Customer Service Department, 5500 Central Avenue, Boulder, CO 80301 (303-444-3541). All prices are subject to change and do not include postage. VISA and MasterCard accepted.

SAIS
REVIEW

VOLUME 7, NUMBER 1
WINTER–SPRING 1987

THE POLITICS OF TERRORISM

Building an Antiterrorist Consensus
GEORGE BUSH

The Uses and Abuses of Terrorism
GARY G. SICK

The Reagan Doctrine: Containment's Last Stand?
ROGER D. HANSEN

Israel: Politics and the Peace Process
SAMUEL W. LEWIS

The PLO: Peace or Self-Preservation?
AARON DAVID MILLER

Hussein's Constraints, Jordan's Dilemma
ARTHUR DAY

Reagan and the Middle East
MARTIN INDYK

MORE THAN A JOURNAL, A RESOURCE!

**THE JOHNS HOPKINS FOREIGN POLICY INSTITUTE
SCHOOL OF ADVANCED INTERNATIONAL STUDIES
1740 MASSACHUSETTS AVENUE, N.W.
WASHINGTON, D.C. 20036**